BUILDING PERSONAL WEALTH FROM INSIDE OUT

ATTRACTING MONEY, HUMAN & MATERIAL RESOURCES THE NATURAL WAY

Goke Akinola

BUILDING PERSONAL WEALTH FROM INSIDE OUT

ISBN: 978-978-964-867-2

Published by:
Geaworth Consult
Plot 9A, Road 3, Ikota Villa Etate,
Lekki, Lagos.

For more information contact:
Email: gokeget@yahoo.com
Phone: 234 (0) 806 292 9176, 234 (0) 708 142 2110.
Website: www.gokeakinola.com

Produced by:
King's Delight Field Ventures
1, Tenibegiloju Street, Iyana-Ipaja, Lagos, Nigeria.
E-mail: kingsdfieldv@gmail.com
Phone: 234 (0) 803 304 1910, 234 (0) 809 841 1965.

Table of Contents

Dedication

Dedicated to Africans of my generation, especially those who were not born with golden spoons in their mouths

Acknowledgment

A tree does not make a forest. Whatever I am, some people have contributed to my success, I am grateful to them. To Pastor B.M.G Amosa, on whose table I found the magazine that changed my orientation right from my school days, it all started from you. To Deacon Shola Atofarati and his family, my companions in the journey of self-actualization, I acknowledge your friendship and support. To Reverend Sam Adeyemi and the Leadership of Daystar Christian Centre, Lagos, where I have received daily spiritual enlightenment, inspiration and moral support, you are most wonderful. As always, I acknowledge Elder Felix Eze who taught me the rudiments of entrepreneurship.

To Sunday Higemeh, Enrico Abutu, Ayodele Komolafe and Fadilat Baruwa, all of Mainstreet Microfinance Bank, who assisted in the typing and proof reading of the manuscript, I appreciate you all. I acknowledge specific people on the Board of Mainstreet Microfinance Bank, particularly Pastor Dan-Habu Bulus, Mr. Olayinka Adebiyi, Mr. Oladayo Afolabi and Mrs. Helen Sule, you all have supported me and provided me with unique opportunities to practice some of the principles of success even at the work place. To Mr. Femi Adegbami who has always supported me with career and personal life advice; thank you for always being there for me. To my consultant, Mr Segun Mamora, I say thank you.

To my wife Joy and my children Adeola and Adewale, whose roles make my life's journey interesting, you are my world of happiness.

Introduction

In 2004, I got the idea of how to break the hold of poverty by the application of a number of success principles. In 2008 I got the idea to put the principles in a book form. By then, I had the basic principles very clear in my mind. To date, I have invested more than nine years of observation, verification and practice of some of the basic principles taught in this book. I can confirm to you that they work. Among the principles were the ones I had known and practiced before 2008. However, the idea of documenting them for others to learn from was not there until then. I am one of the people that had limited chances of success in life.

Even among my siblings, the trajectory of my life has been very different from theirs. Thirteen years in the village led to academic setback for me, compared with my siblings who lived in the city. My later years in the secondary school were with serious financial difficulties. The years in the Polytechnic were even more difficult. In my early days in the Polytechnic, I supported myself with farming activities. In the final year, I hawked foot mats and worked in a quarry site in Ibadan. Before then, there was a time one of my friends (now late) and I had to survive by hunting and selling bush animals. This is not in any way discounting the supportive roles played by a number of people along the line. However, I have come to learn that the most critical factor in any journey of life is the person concerned himself. Other people and resources will always come to assist you either to succeed or to fail.

At a time, my mother worked as a nanny with a family in Surulere. The family later moved to Lekki area of Lagos, shortly after my mother had left them. She used to follow them to the site when the house was under construction. Years later, she almost fainted the day she discovered that our new house is now in the same neighborhood that her former employers were once building their new house. There was also a time she worked as a restaurant attendant in Festac. She was with my younger sister as a co-worker in that restaurant. Mother and daughter were employees of the same person.

Today, the story is different. Anyone can decide to change his financial and social status. The advantage I have is to have practiced many of the principles of financial abundance taught in this book. I have been able to move from the theory to the practical aspect of the financial success principles in this book. I can guarantee, those principles work.

As a child, I was told poverty is not a disease. We were made to believe that possession of money for personal use is a function of luck- meant for a lucky few. Today, many still hold the view that lack of money only means that you are unlucky and that, cannot be your fault.

Nothing can be farther from the truth. Considering the reality of today's society, acquisition of money and material resources is very fundamental to healthy life. Successful living is almost impossible in our society of today without money to spend. However, a fundamental truth is that all humans like any other creature are created with natural innate resources that can be deployed for generation of all the resources necessary for survival and thriving. Nature also positions each person in such a way that our immediate environment is littered with things and circumstances that can work together in generation of money and materials for our successful living. These internal and external resources answer only to principles. They answer to personal and collective choices. This book explores those principles in practical terms.

This book is one in a series of books on principles that enable anybody to build financial strength and secure lasting financial freedom. The first two books in the series are titled "Poverty Has A Cure" and "How to Activate Your Personal Money Instinct" respectively. This is therefore the third in the series.

"We are all affected by money, no matter who we are or where we live or what we do. Money like time, is a common denominator we share. Most people need money to buy food, which is necessary to sustain life, so they are intertwined whether we choose to believe it or not.

Money will affect your life. My theory is that if something is going to affect your life, it's best to know as much as you can about it. Will you be able to find time to invest in your financial education?" Donald J. Trump

True financial success involves personal choices. You cannot be rich as a result of economic accident. Success results only when opportunity is greeted with preparedness. Any fortune that comes to you without your preparedness is the fortune that will soon disappear. To be financially successful, you must have financial success as one of your chief goals. Your personal choices have the ability to activate the personal power from within you with which you can attain financial abundance. The personal power from the inside of you has the force to attract all that you require for the attainment of your chief goals. All that you need are available in terms of materials, people and opportunities. They are all available in the world around you. Personal choices draw you to all that you need and draw all that you need to you. Personal choices also empower you to be able to develop habits that naturally attract money making opportunities to you. These are part of natural laws upon which our universe operates.

Reading this book may be one of the most critical preparatory steps in your quest to achieving and sustaining financial and material abundance.

Chapter One

Wealthy Environment

ACTION MOTIVATORS

Even with the great deal of emphasis that has been placed on the importance of thinking, no one can become rich only by thinking endlessly. Thinking must lead to action. The value of a thought is in the type of actions it produces in us. Until you have evaluated the actions of people, you will never notice any difference between persons whose actions are ruled by thoughts and others whose actions are ruled by feelings.

In between your thoughts and actions, is what I refer to as action motivators. By action motivators I mean the underlining factors of the outcomes of your life. They are the innate reasons for life's successes or failures. They are the unannounced reasons for the results we are getting in each of our life's endeavours. These action motivators both shape our thoughts and our thoughts shape them. They influence our feelings, thoughts and actions. More importantly, they draw from our thoughts and our thoughts draw from them. The mastering of these action motivators is very critical to success in life. They are the ultimate determinants of financial success or failure.

I have adopted the following classification of action motivators.

1. ENVIRONMENT
2. KNOWLEDGE
3. EXPERIENCE
4. BELIEFS
5. VALUES
6. CHOICES
7. ACTIONS

The way you master and handle the interplay of the above will determine the outcome of your life. By obtaining informations about you along the seven areas above, I can predict your financial future almost with scientific accuracy. Let me briefly discuss each of the success motivators. They are also called action motivators. This is because what actually produces success is a combination of actions. Actions are also final results of a combination and interplay of other factors as listed above and discussed below.

1. ENVIRONMENT

This refers to the totality of everything around you. It involves the human and non - human elements you relate with through your five senses. Your dominant environment shapes your thoughts. It has to do with the combination of what you see, hear, touch, feel, smell and taste regularly. Each of these elements has different levels of impact on us as humans but the totality of them has an aggregated effect on the outcomes of our lives.

We all draw information from our environment both consciously and unconsciously. The type of information you draw and how you draw it will surely shape your future in line with the nature of such information. It is the responsibility of an individual to determine the information he wants to draw and where to draw it from.

The most critical elements of our environment are our fellow men. This is because they have the ability to influence us more than any other element around us. Human actions and activities are products of the mind, which is why they impact the minds of other humans tremendously.

Attempting to be different from the combination of what you see and relate with every day is a very difficult task. If you live among poor people and you listen to them regularly, the best outcome you should expect of your life should be poverty, all things being equal. Of course, it is possible for you to see a ray of light afar off. But the only action that can rescue you from the domination of poverty is to draw closer to the ray of light you can see afar off. If you live your life always around criminals particularly where they are allowed to shape your opinion, you can rightly be expected to commit crime some day. The best option available to you is to do everything humanly possible to get out of the company of criminals. Evil communication corrupts good manner. Just as good communication also builds good manner.

The good news is that anyone can decide the type of environment he wants to live in. You can also create the environment you want around you. As an adult, I can determine what I want to listen to and who I want to listen to. I can determine who my friends will be. I can determine whose opinions will shape my thoughts and influence my actions. It only requires my critical analysis of people around me and decision as to who I wants to gravitate towards. That is where the power of the mind is very critical. Even your non – human environment is very important. The type of house you live in has a way of shaping your financial future. The type of school you attended influences your future not only by the type of academic knowledge impacted on you but also by the type of infrastructure available and the quality of people you related with. They all determine your exposure and your exposure affects the capacity of your mind. The type of company you work is important not only by how much salary it pays but by the totality of its policies, culture, practices, values and the quality of people it keeps. The boss you work with is an important factor in determining the legitimate outcome you can expect of your future.

If you joined a company or you are planning to join a company, look at the lives of the senior people in that company. Look at the lives of the major decision makers in that company. Determine if there are at least three senior individuals you wish your future would be like their present state of living and life styles. Look at your church and determine whether there are people you want your life to be like their's someday.

You need to do this analysis specific to different areas of your life. Put all the answers together to arrive at an aggregate or average that will tell you whether or not you are in the right place. About nine years ago I made a decision on the type of church I can belong to as a member. There are pastors whose values promote poverty. They preach and live in such a way to give members the impression that poverty is a virtue. Some live their lives in a way that suggests that being rich is a matter of luck or destiny. They console their members by giving them the impression that the rich people around are all thieves and criminals. I can never be a member of such a congregation. I belonged to such a congregation in the past but not anymore. I took that decision without anybody specifically prompting me. I acted based on my personal analysis of events and my then environment. I thank God I did.

"I don't think God cares if you are rich or poor. God loves you any way. But if you want to be rich, then choose your church and your preacher carefully." Rich Dad

This is not the only factor that determines which church someone should belong. There are many other very important factors. But for me, this is certainly one of the factors. There are people who think the religious congregation to which they belong has nothing to do with their finances. They are wrong. Everything around you has something to do with your finances. Your church, your neighborhood, your spouse, your children, your friends, your office or company where you work and the likes affect your finances in different degrees. Don't assume church matters are spiritual and money is material. Money is both spiritual and material. And man is as spiritual as he is physical.

INTERNAL VS EXTERNAL ENVIRONMENT

I must add that there is external environment and there is

internal environment. Your internal environment is the combination of thoughts and pictures that dominate your mind. Your mind is a world of its own which must be deliberately decorated with the type of thoughts and pictures compatible with the type of outcome you want for your life. It is everyone's personal responsibility to create the desirable environment in his or her mind. You must also know that the internal environment is more important than the external environment. Your internal environment is a strong factor that determines your external environment. By critical observation you will discover that your dominant thought determines the kind of people that comes in contact with you and the ones you come in contact with. Your dominant thoughts influence what happens to you and what happens around you.

The good news is that even when you are in prison custody, you may not be able to set yourself free physically yet you can set yourself free in the mind, because even in the prison, you can decide the type of things you listen to; you can determine the kind of people you want to associate with. Even in the prison, there are different types of people. You can determine the types of songs you want to sing. All these and many more are factors of internal environment that will ultimately transform any body's external environment. In prison you can determine the type of books you want to read. You can also decide not to read at all. Internal environments are of stronger force because the mind is the center of your being. A major pointer to this is also in the

Bible verses that said "**Keep your heart with all diligence for out of it are the issues of life**" and "**As a man thinks in his heart so is he**". Don't worry about your future. Be committed to shaping your mind. And your mind, will shape your future.

Your external environment influences your internal environment. In the same vein, your internal environment influences your external environment over time. But the major driver of your life is your internal environment. This is because your internal environment does not only affect your external environment but it also affects your entire life. You have more control on your internal environment than the external environment. You don't need permission from anyone to change your internal environment. Whatever your internal environment is today will be reflected in your entire life over time. Your entire life includes your external environment. It includes the location, the society and the type of things that will happen to you and around you every time. It includes your feelings, thoughts and actions.

The rich man of today has actually become rich in his mind a long time ago before the riches or wealth you see today began to manifest. Where money comes to you by any form of economic accident, such money will soon disappear because your internal environment is not compatible with it. Anyone can decide to change his internal environment. The types of books you find in my library today is what I know is difficult to find with many of my peers. I invested in books and other knowledge materials even when my income was still meager. I do my best to baptize my mind in the knowledge from these resources from time to time. It is then possible for me to live above my immediate physical environment per time.

Anywhere I am, it is not unusual for me to be a star in that particular location at any time. This is because knowledge stands you out. I have unique perspectives on many issues of life; this has reflected in my career, family and even spiritual life. It was mentioned in one of my earlier books that I attended local schools in the primary and secondary school days. I had also mentioned how at different times I have found myself in places where people who graduated from better equipped and more reputable schools had to look up to me. Attending any of these renowned institutions would probably have given me better advantages and speed in many ways. However, that was not possible by some acts of fate. I have to work on my mind in so many ways to overcome all the disadvantages of my early years.

When advising young people, I discover that there are loads of excuses that people give for not achieving success. The most common I can readily remember are lack of money or capital, no connection or social network and marginalization of some sort. Most people who complain of marginalization talk on tribal marginalization and gender marginalization. Others call it discrimination. Ladies usually talk of sexual harassment. Most claim that a particular individual or employers denied them jobs because they refused sexual advances from such individuals. In my opinion, many of these things are just figments of those ladies' imaginations. At some other times, the harassment, discrimination and marginalization are actually real. My advice to ladies is that they should ensure that they have skills and knowledge that stand them out. Instead of employers giving you conditions, you will give the employers conditions. It is a principle that will always work. Knowledge breeds confidence and courage. When you have done that, be ready to walk away from anyone that will ask for any compromise that is not acceptable to you. Be ready to move or continue to work on yourself. I have had to write my employment letter a number of time. I have also had to write reference letter for my self a number of times. In each case, the authorizing person will only have to sign off.

There is always a place for anyone who is a problem solver. Develop yourself to be a problem solver. The would-be employer that is demanding for intimate relationship from you is doing so because he feels you are indebted to him for giving you a job. There is a level of knowledge and skill you display that your employer will feel indebted to you for accepting to work for him. This kind of thing happens first on the inside before it manifests on the outside. Your taking up a job should go beyond being able to pay your bills. Your primary reason should be to add value to people, organizations and the society. It must be to solve some human problems.

When we were in the universities or polytechnics, we were all busy imagining an office where we would someday be paid some huge amount of money as salary. Whereas, we were supposed to imagine how we will provide solution to certain human problems. When you solve problems; money has no choice than to come to you.

2. KNOWLEDGE

This talks of the totality of the informative impacts of our environment on us. Environment produces some sort of knowledge and awareness in us. Here we are not referring to formal knowledge alone. It is the sum total of the awareness that you have about yourself and the world around you. The impact of all the animate and inanimate components of our environment on us is to bring up in us some kind of consciousness and awareness.

Our academic environment provides in us academic knowledge. Your social environment will provide social knowledge or awareness in you. People's backgrounds leave some impact on them that can last for entire life time.

Another perspective to the discussion on knowledge is your expectation. As an individual, there is something you expect from other people. You have expectation even from you to yourself as well as from and to other people. You equally have expectations from and towards the society at large. There is a content of people's behavior and actions in life that is a function of their expectation. The root of such expectation is our environment both at present and in the past. Because of what I know about myself and the world around me, what I know about my society and other societies outside mine, there is an expectation I have of myself and other people. The sum total of the expectations influences my actions and reactions. There is a reason I will never behave like an average Lagos bus conductor; because we are not products of the same environment. This same factor moderates my reaction to the behavior of a Lagos bus conductor. The two of us are not running on the same knowledge. We don't have the same exposure.

Before you can conveniently change your actions and ultimately change your results in life, you need to change your environment. Your changed environment will produce in you, new set of knowledge. When you know better, you will live better. New knowledge will certainly lead to new experience.

When you know better, you will live better. Information brings transformation. Negative information also leads to deformation. It is a principle of life. The quality of your life is determined by the level of positive awareness you have in specific important areas of life.

3. EXPERIENCE

By experience we refer to the events in your life, your responsibility or reaction to them and the lessons or conclusions you draw from them. Every experience leaves a conclusion in you that positions you for a future event. That is the reason it is believed in many circles that experience is the best teacher. If that is the case, bad experiences should teach us to avoid their types in the future. All past and present experiences should actually make us better for future decisions and actions. In a way, the events of the past are parts of history but their impact on us is the experience. It is also a common knowledge that history repeats itself. That means in a way, experiences can also repeat themselves. In the first place, it is very possible to reproduce an experience. It is possible to repeat history intentionally. That is, the repeat is not an accident. This is usually applicable to good history and desirable experiences. All you need to do is to repeat the actions and you will have the experience.

But there are also repeat of bad history and undesirable experiences, there are people who repeat the same mistake over and over again. The truth is that our experiences are products of our environment and knowledge. They are a reflection of your environment and knowledge. If you wish to change your experience (things that happen to you) consider changing your environment and your knowledge.

We have discussed earlier and made it abundantly clear that your environment is more than just a location. It is the sum total of the things and humans that you relate with regularly and their impacts on you. Also remember that you have both the internal environment as well as the external environment. Just like your body and the senses can relate and interact with people and other elements around you, so also your mind has the power to relate. The relational power of the mind is based on the use of what the mind picks from the senses and those things that the mind generates on its own by default. Your experience is the blend of your numerous exposures. It has the power to shape your expectation, mentality and mind set. The good news is that you can consciously orchestrate or influence the type of experiences and exposures you want to have.

Change your internal and external environment; then change the knowledge you have by drawing new knowledge from your new and better environment. Then you will begin to have new and better experiences. It is also possible that the environment that was good enough for you in the past is no longer good for today. Learn to change your environment not only because the current environment is not good but also because you have outgrown that environment.

There was a particular area where I lived some years back. Even though I was a very quiet person, the people in the area saw me as a shining light in their midst. They also tried to appreciate my generosity especially towards the youths. However, at some point it appeared their expectations and requests from me were becoming too much for me. It also appeared that my reactions to certain issues were not compatible with their expectation. No one ever told me this, but I was smart enough to have perceived this myself. During that period, I had a baby. The people naturally expected I was going to throw a big party. Just because I had borne part of the financial burden of the naming ceremony (ies) of some of them in the past. I had seen how many of them over stretched themselves financially on things that were not compulsory, like naming ceremonies. I even saw people who begged me to help them with money to buy goats for naming ceremonies. Often times I got frustrated when I discovered that the person I raised money for to buy goat, blocked public roads with canopies and hired plastic chairs on the naming day.

And so, I felt it was necessary I show them that such ceremonies, though not bad, are not compulsory to the extent of having to beg or borrow money to organize them. I was also not comfortable with the idea of people blocking public roads for any ceremony. Therefore, when my baby was born I refused to throw any party. The money I would have used to throw a party was used instead to create a fixed deposit investment in the name of the baby. While some of them were pleasantly surprised at what I did, others especially the youths who had expected a lot of eating and drinking felt very disappointed and disgruntled. These groups were of the opinion that I did not want to share my resources with people. They felt I had money but did not want other people to benefit from my money. They suddenly forgot how much I had done for many of them in the past, both individually and collectively.

Even though I had my plans to move out of that area, the events that followed actually made me to leave the area earlier than planned. On a normal day, no one could have expected armed robbery attack on my house. This is because even the notorious boys in the area, used to get gifts of money and other items severally from me, from time to time. These boys usually have informations about any crime that happened or would happen in the area. To everybody's surprise, there was an armed robbery attack and they vandalized one of my cars and made away with the critical parts of the car.

Few months later, there was another attack in which another car of mine was vandalized. This time around, the armed robbers were with my car in the middle of the night for more than three hours. I even saw and flashed torch light at them and they threatened to shoot me with a gun. This was in the night of the 23rd to 24th of December of that year. We packed out of the house the day after.

It would have been wrong for me to remain in that place and hoping the experience would change. Of course, I was also aware that my status had gone beyond that area long before any of the incidences. It is very difficult to see any truly rich person, living among very poor people. The reality is that, there can never be compatibility. Good life is the combination of good experiences. Bad life is the one full of bad experiences. The truth is that you can orchestrate your experiences in life. Your duty is to determine the kind of environment and knowledge you take into your mind.

Change your expectations of yourself and of other people. Give to life what you expect life to give back to you. Do your best to make good things happen to other people. As a principle of life, others will work to make good things happen to you. When you remain among poor people, it is not likely you will become rich from among them. This is because the totality of your experiences and exposures will be dominated by poverty experience and history. This in turn will breed poverty mentality in you. It was the wife of J. F. Kennedy, Former President of the U. S. that said if she ever got broke, what she would do is to go to a 5 Star Hotel and buy a bottle of Champagne and sit down to drink it where she can listen to the conversation of the rich people for a few hours. Think about that. The emphasis is on the tremendous impact of sharing from the experience and conversation of rich people. If you allow the rich to shape your opinion, you are very likely to become rich in a matter of time. If you want to become a millionaire, talk to billionaires, you will get there quickly.

In other words, if the poor shape your opinion you are most likely going to become poor in a matter of time.

"What you think about is what you bring about"

Each economic class has words that reflect it and define it: Rich people use rich words, middle class people use middle class words, and poor people use poor words.

Select the five people you listen to most of the time. Add the wealth of the five people together and divide your result by five. The result of this exercise is what you will likely become financially in a matter of time if you continue long enough in that setting. For those people who are comfortable being local champions, it is reasonable you do this same exercise. Those poor people around you will rub off on you in a matter of time. Their poverty will rub off on your wealth over time. Their poverty will dilute your wealth over time. At first, their opinions and views will dilute yours without you taking note. You will gradually begin to share from their mentality. That will create a kind of internal and external environment in you which will in turn affect the outcome of your financial life. It will get to produce enough poverty experiences in you which will later shape your beliefs about money. The chain continues.

4. BELIEFS

"Beliefs are the core of who we are, what we do and the

success that we acquire" Ty Bennett in "True Definition of Belief".

In 1948, Claude M. Bristol wrote a wonderful book entitled the "Magic of Believing". In his book he explained that there is one common strand woven throughout the many cultures and religions he investigated. All people whether primitive or civilized have shared a particular philosophy that is central to their culture. People of all ages have subscribed to the idea that if you believe that something will happen, it will take place. It is the power of belief that causes things to happen in our lives.

Most people define beliefs as inward convictions, a feeling of certainty about what something means. They are what you hold dear and are rooted deeply within. A belief is both mental and emotional. It is embedded in the mind and in the heart. Your beliefs will dictate your action. If you believe in a cause, you will fight for it.

What is belief? Belief is "an acceptance that something exists or is true, especially one without proof"

One cannot overemphasize the importance of belief in human life. Success in life or lack of it is a function of your belief. It is practically impossible for man to live or do anything without belief. There cannot exit such vacuum in man. The absence of belief in a particular thing is the presence of your belief in the opposite of it. If you don't believe that you can do or become a particular thing, you will actually not be able to do or become that thing. Your lack of belief in the possibility of that thing is not an absence of faith. Rather, it is the presence of faith or belief in the opposite. Your lack of belief in its possibility is the presence of your belief in its impossibility. Belief is so fundamental to human existence that you cannot live without it. There cannot be a vacuum about it. You cannot be neutral on this.

When it comes to movement from poverty to wealth, belief is very fundamental. You must not only believe that you can be rich but you must come to a level where you believe that you are rich already. The difficulty many people face in this area is that they wonder how normal it is for someone to believe the opposite of what is obvious. In reality, this is the difference between the rich and the poor. The truly rich people see the wealth before it comes in the physical. This is not just a religious theory; it is a principle of life.

The secret is in you being able to identify wealth in other forms than in currency notes. You must understand that wealth has both the intrinsic and extrinsic forms. The physical cash and other tangible assets are the extrinsic forms of wealth. In reality, wealth must exist in the intrinsic form before it can find expression in the extrinsic form. If you have passed through the site of the ongoing Eko Atlantic City Project, you will appreciate this is a massive expression of wealth. The project has consumed billions of dollars. It will still consume multiples of what has been put into it so far. You must however realize that the project first existed in someone or some peoples' mind. It later existed on paper. Later it came to physical expression. All the people that invested their hard earned money in that place did not invest in the physical structures that we now see; they all invested in what was on paper. The truth is that they actually saw it as real then; just as we can see today. They were able to believe in it and then they can invest or participate in it.

The most important thing to note here is the fact that your belief is a product of your environment, your knowledge and your experience. Every man also has the power to change his or her belief. If you change what you see and hear regularly and the kind of people you associate with, your belief will change effortlessly.

The belief of the rich man is different from that of the poor man. They are actually opposite in nature; the two of them believe different things about themselves and the world around them. The rich man believes in riches and therefore he attracts it; the rich man believes in prosperity and he also attracts what he believes. The resources everyone needs to succeed are available in the world. In fact, by nature, they are available in places close to you or places you can reach if you so decide. The force that pulls those resources to you and pushes you to them is your belief.

Your belief today is a product of your environment up until now, your current knowledge and sum total of your experiences so far. You can change your environment. You can change your knowledge; you can change your experience. A new belief will naturally emerge in you in line with your new reality.

5. VALUES

Values "*are the guiding principles that dictate behavior and action". They are the principles or standards of behavior; or one's judgment of what is important in life*."

Your values are the basic expression of your beliefs. They are the basic assumptions which form the basis of your ethical actions. They determine what you attach importance to and the amount of importance you attach to them.

A man's values are fundamental in determining the outcome of his life. Your values are major factors in the determination of the application of your energy, time and other resources. The outcomes of your life can only be a reflection of how you have applied resources available to you. For instance, time is about the most valuable resource God has made available to all of us. Interestingly, the same amount of time is made available to each and every individual. This is one of the things that nature has endowed both the rich and the poor equally with. However, the values of the rich and the poor as far as time is concerned are not the same.

The rich believes time to be the most valuable resources while the poor attach little or no value to it. The rich man values it; the rich man is very careful about how he spends his time. The poor man does otherwise. The truly rich man attaches more value to time than physical cash. He is well aware that the real producer of the physical money and other assets is time properly spent. The rich man will happily spend N50, 000 buying return ticket to travel from Lagos to Abuja in three to four hours. The poor man will feel he has saved money by taking bus for N10,000 to and from Abuja spending three days to do what he can otherwise do in four hours.

Recently, I was on a two weeks vacation. I could not travel out of the country because of certain things that came up after concluding the arrangements for my leave. I had to stay indoor studying for most of the leave period. There was this young man that kept coming to look for me for some financial assistance. There was no appointment. He would only come and wait at our gate around 7am hoping to meet me any time I stepped out to go to the office. Unfortunately for him, I did not even step out of the house for more than 5 days. Whenever members of my family stepped out of the gate, they would meet him at the gate. When they told him that I was still sleeping and they were not ready to interrupt my sleep, the young man still waited for hours at the gate hoping that I would eventually come out of the gate. He left after waiting for hours at the gate. He repeated the same thing the following morning. It took days before he was able to meet me on a Sunday afternoon. I compared the amount of money he was expecting from me with the amount of time he had spent at my gate for those number of days. It was not worth it.

A poor man can wait for 24 hours to be able to get N500 (Five Hundred Naira Only) from you. The simple explanation is this; based on his value system, 24hours of his life does not worth more than N500. A rich man knows that 24hours of his life thoughtfully applied will generate multiples of N500. The rich man wants to make profitable use of his 24hours a day. He also wants to buy more time from other people to add to his own. That is the reason he will employ other people and pay them for their time. The rich man knows that he is rich because of the profitable use of his own time and the additional time he has been able to buy from other people. That is why all truely rich people are all employers of labour. I doubt if anyone can truly be wealthy working as an employee. Even with the best of brain, you are limited to what you can achieve within the 24hours of a day as an employee.

Value is a major determinant of the outcome of our lives. As it is in application to time, it is applicable to every other aspect of our lives. The rich man has developed a set of wealth building and sustaining values. Consistent practice of these values can make anyone wealthy in a matter of time.

We must also note that values are not natural gifts. They are cultivated and developed. The poor man's problem is his set of poverty breeding values. The day he changes them is the day he starts the journey to wealth. Among others, you need to have the right value of time, for relationship and for knowledge. Have the right value for hard work, habit of saving money, truthfulness, trust and so on. Those values imbibed and practiced over time will result in success in virtually every area of our lives. Instead of bothering yourself about how to make quick money, develop wealth building values. The practice of these values will give you all the money in a matter of time. Right money values will also guaranttee peace of mind.

Watch the lives of truely rich people around; their values which are always fundamentally different from those of their poor fellows' are very obvious to see. Someone's value is best noticed in the way he applies his available resources. You apply resources based on your order of importance or priority. This is done almost unconsciously. It is done without taking note of it. But it is done anyway and it matters. We must also note that values are not in isolation. They are products of our environment, knowledge, experiences and beliefs. As stated earlier, values are the most basic expression of our beliefs.

6. CHOICES

There are many choices we have to make in life. Some

choices are made once and they affect the course of our entire lives. Others have to be made over and over again. The truth is that the quality of a person's life cannot be better than the sum total of the choices he has made in the past. Our choices are the offshoots of our values. The true reflection of someone's values is in the type of choices he makes. These choices are also products of the blend of our environment, knowledge, experiences, beliefs and values.

Most poor people are people who have not discovered that wealth is a choice just like poverty is a choice. Many poor folks assume or believe that God in heaven reserves the choice for Himself as to who will be rich and who will remain poor in this world. They present it in a way that suggests that God does not have criteria for selecting who will be rich or who will be poor. The truth is that for you to be truly successful, you must decide to do so. Your choice is involved. For you to be truly rich, you must decide to be rich with the determination to pay the price. God is involved in the affairs of men. However, God will never make that important choice for anyone. It must also be noted that not making a choice to be rich is automatically making a choice to be poor. There cannot be a vacuum in this regard. You may get money by accident or luck, but you cannot sustain it by accident. Personal choice is involved.

Any money that comes to the hands of a man who has not made a choice to be rich is the money that will soon disappear. In fact, the Bible says such money or riches have wings with which it will soon fly away.

Choices also do not exist in isolation. They are products of the environment, knowledge, experience, beliefs and values.

7. ACTIONS

These are the ultimate determinants of the results of our lives. Actions are the most visible aspects of the success motivators; they are what everyone around can see. But they are actually the final expression of the impact of our environment, knowledge, experiences, beliefs, values and choices. They are very easy to see because they involve the use of our physical bodies and the senses. Actions are the most visible aspects of the success motivators because they touch other people. Actions are real result drivers in human lives.

Finally, it must be noted that in real life, these success motivators do not have to be arranged in the order they have been presented here for them to be easy. What matters is your consciousness and awareness of these fundamental truths and your application of the principles around them.

There is this saying that "actions speak louder than words". Actions truly speak. But the deeper truth is that actions only echo what the combination of our environment, knowledge, experience, beliefs, values and choices are saying. Actions are the final expressions of the above fundamental factors of human behaviors.

You can change the results of your life by changing your actions. To change your actions, you must change your choices. For your choices to change your values have to change. Values are products of beliefs, to change values, you must change the beliefs that drive them. Your beliefs develop from your experience. They have to change before your beliefs will change. To change your experience you must first change your knowledge. Your knowledge derives from your environment. Change your environment and your knowledge will automatically change.

In conclusion, your major success in life will be predicated around your ability to gain control over and change your internal and external environment.

Chapter Two

Dominant Awareness

WHEN A PROPHET COMES TO TOWN

As I walked along in a neighborhood in Ogbomosho on a particular day, in company of my uncle. He was one of the financially successful men in the town. I had been privileged to learn some business and life lessons from him.

The neighborhood was on the outskirt of the city. A young evangelist in the town has just built a worship facility in front of which we were passing that day. On a lighter note, we were discussing about the impact of the young evangelist's activities in the city as at that time. Along the line, I expressed concern about the new building. My concern was that the new hall of meeting was built in such a place that was so remote and far from the city center. This was after we both acknowledged the impact of the various programmes organized by the religious organization led by this young evangelist. He had just relocated his church to this newly built facility in the remote area.

"It should have been located in a more central place in the town"; I said.

My uncle's reaction shocked me and opened a new line of thinking in me. He answered with a question. "Have you ever seen any powerful prophet come to town?" he asked. I looked at his face with the kind of expression that told him I had never thought about that. He further asked me to look around and see if there is any powerful prophet that targets establishing his ministry in the center of the city. He stated in the affirmative that one way to know a powerful prophet is that he would site his ministry in a remote place. He gave many examples locally and abroad. In addition, he told me that usually, cities grow in the direction of such powerful prophets. They normally open up new locations and other people follow in their direction naturally.

I have applied time and thought in the last two decades to confirm the truth of what my uncle stated as a principle. I have also discovered that even when a major church is located in the city because of the cosmopolitan nature of a place like Lagos, you discover that they bring something out of the place that thousands of people never thought was possible to come out of such a place. In addition, those that started in town soon move to the outskirt of the city as the congregation increases. They open up new places and the Society naturally follow. Sometimes they takeover an abandoned piece of property and make surprises out of it. Trully great people are always ready to break need grounds

DOMINANT AWARENESS PRINCIPLE

Your life is a reflection of the thoughts that occupy your mind most of the time. The type of life someone lives is a reflection of the dominant thoughts in that persons mind. It is a reflection of the person's regular thoughts. Your personality is the totality of the most dominant thoughts in your mind always. The rich man's mind is dominated by thoughts of wealth. The poor man's mind is dominated by thoughts of poverty. **The poor man does not think of poverty because he is poor. Rather, he is poor because he thinks of poverty. The rich man does not think of riches just because he is rich. Rather, he is rich because he thinks of riches and wealth.** The outcome of a person's life is a function of the type of thoughts in that person's mind and the persistency of those thoughts in his mind. It is the thought that produces the reality and not the other way round.

There are hundreds of stories of men and women who dared what most people dreaded and so became leaders in their generations. This type of stories cut across different spheres of life. It is not limited to business, religion or politics. This is also a function of the same factors. It is usually a function of **power consciousness**. People who dare what others don't dare are people with the dominant awareness that they have what others don't have. They see what others don't see in that particular sphere of life.

This power is usually of three dimensions.

First, it is the presence of that thing that you have that others around you do not have. That in itself is power. It is called advantage in the corporate world. It may be a location advantage, time advantage, information advantage, size advantage or any of such things. It drives and motivates you to be able to do what others and even you will not attempt to do under normal circumstances. Sometimes that power is special knowledge, it may be the possession of money or other valuable resources. At other times it may be some kind of social network or political association you belong that fuels in you the unusual courage, drive and confidence. It may even be some spiritual power. It may be faith in yourself or some other things. For another person, it may be a kind of strong faith in his personal ability. It may also be a strong confidence in your social connection.

Watch carefully, you will discover there is a natural courage, drive or confidence which is a direct product of any or a combination of the above.

The **second** dimension of this power is the awareness or the consciousness of the power itself. There is power that naturally flows from a position of authority. There is an additional power that flows from your personal awareness and consciousness of the power attached to the position of authority. Knowledge they say is power. The application of knowledge is also a greater power. Consciousness is more than just knowledge. It is consciousness when the knowledge gives you an unusual drive to get something done. It is consciousness when that knowledge directs your actions on related matters.

The prophets that clear the forest to establish themselves are usually driven by either the power they carry or the power they believe they carry. They are also driven by the awareness of such power rightly or wrongly. This is not to attest to the genuineness or otherwise of any of those individuals or their ministries.

This principle works regardless of the nature of power you carry. It works regardless of whether the power is from God or from the devil. What matters is either you carry something that the majority of others do not carry or you believe you carry something that others around you do not carry or a combination of both. It may be that you know or see what others around you do not know or see. Or you simply believe that you see what others do not see or know. Whatever is the source of your power or knowledge does not matter, the principle will still work. The final outcome may be different depending on the source of the power or authenticity of the knowledge. The end may justify whether someone was actually right or wrong. But at the beginning, the presence of special power, special knowledge or vision and the consciousness of them feel the same. Special information can give you an unusual advantage in your industry.

I have both read and listened to life stories of a number of Christian Ministries that support the working and reality of this principle.

One of such was the story about how Pastor W. F. Kumuyi of The Deeper Life Bible Church was able to take possession of the place where the Headquarters of the church stands today in Gbagada area of Lagos. History has it that the particular area was a thick forest believed to be occupied by a dreaded python. The locals and the villagers believed that the python was a god which some of them actually worshiped. To the surprise of the people, a pastor and his church came around and offered to buy the dreaded forest. The day the forest was to be cleared for the church building project to start was full of drama. It was a life story of man, fighting with a python that had actually become an object of worship of a set of people. Today, a masterpiece and an architectural wonder sits on that portion of land, which is the International Headquarters of the Deeper Life Bible Church.

I recently drove through the Lekki-Epe Express way of Lagos. There is a particular religious ground called Bethel Church Wonder City. The record was that the structure was built when that area was just like a forest, which people never imagined could be inhabited by humans. Even though, the ministry is today a shadow of its old self, it was the church that opened up the Ajah area of Lagos where thousands of people now live. The pastor of the church was reported to be one of the first private individuals to own private aircrafts in Nigeria decades ago.

Winners Chapel moved to the Canaan Land when majority of people never imagined a worship centre could be built in such a remote forest. Former President Olusegun Obasanjo went to that area even decades before that time to acquire the place where he later established his popular Otta Farm, Bells University of Technology and other major projects today.

There are stories of other great men that did such in the revival era in Europe and America.

Have you ever observed that most rich corporate bodies do the same? They acquire places average people would never think of and make a master piece out of them. Most wealthy individuals do the same. Sometimes it is a swampy area that will take millions of dollars or Naira to be able to make it habitable.

Behind such actions is the power of either money, knowledge or other resources which the carriers are well conscious of. I have been to where former president Ibrahim Babangida built his mansion in Minna. The topography of that place was the one you cannot imagine on a normal day such a piece could come out of it.

When there is resources or specialized knowledge together with personal consciousness of such, those things that would have naturally been disadvantages turn out to become endowments. They take a positive role instead of a negative role. Sometimes it is the fact that you are aware that the majority of the people are in love with you. It is called social capital or goodwill.

This principle has a lot to do with leadership and success in every human endeavor. The presence of any form of specialized power and the consciousness of the possession of such power makes a man stand out among his peers. The consciousness that you can do what majority of people around you cannot do or achieve sets you ahead of others. There is a saying that a man with one eye will certainly be the king in the city of the blind. It also goes with this principle. The man with one eye can do what his other blind friends cannot do. At least, he can see with one eye. He is equally aware of his special ability. His other blind friends are also aware of his special ability among them, and so they submit to him and make him king automatically. Who else could have been the king of the jungle apart from the lion?

"There is a genius in every man and woman, waiting to be brought forth. Every village has its great man or woman; someone to whom all go for advice in time of trouble; someone who is instinctively recognized as being great in wisdom and insight. To such a one the minds of the whole community turn in times of local crises; he is tacitly recognized as being great. He does small things in a great way. He could do great things as well if he did but undertake them; so can any man; so can you.

There are two mental attitudes a man may take. One makes him like a football. It has resilience and reacts strongly when force is applied to it, but it originates nothing; it never acts of itself. There is no power within it. Men of this type are controlled by circumstances and environment; their destinies are decided by things external to themselves. The principle of power within them is never really actived at all. They never speak or act from within.

The other attitude makes man like a flowing spring. Power comes out from the centre of him. He has within him a well of water springing up into everlasting life, he radiates force; he is felt by his environment. The principle of power in him is in constant action. He is self-active. He

hath life in himself" Wallace D. Wattles

The financially intelligent know the need to always have something that puts them ahead of other people. They apply this knowledge in whatever sphere of life they find themselves. When you know what other people do not know in an area of life, you naturally become their leader in that area.

That is the reason why people try to specialize in specific area of human endeavour. Most areas of knowledge today have specialists or professionals. When people with knowledge in that particular area are gathered, the specialist or professional stands out. Ironically thousands of people specialize today without understanding the principles. This lack of understanding makes people not to apply their minds to acquire specialized knowledge; instead, many go for specialized certificates. Whenever you know what others don't know, they will reward you for that knowledge; it is just a matter of time. This is particularly when the knowledge provides solution to their particular problems.

This special knowledge or power and the consciousness of it will always attract money and other resources of life. Each of us is born with certain personal advantages. To succeed we must make conscious efforts to discover such natural personal advantages. Secondly, every body can acquire personal advantages in his or her area of interest. The point is personal advantage is very important for success in life.

KNOWLEDGE WITHOUT CERTIFICATE

I currently run a Law (LLB) program at the National Open University of Nigeria (NOUN). We were already in 300 level before getting to know about the decision of the Nigerian Council of Legal Education not to admit graduates from NOUN to the Nigerian Law School. The reason the Council gave was that the National Open University is a part-time program. Whether that reason was reasonable or genuine enough is an issue for debate. At least we know of a number of legal icons in Nigeria today who studied to become lawyers decades ago via correspondent courses.

My lawyer friend, a first class product of the University of Ibadan expressed his concern for me in a telephone conversation recently. He felt very bad that we may not be allowed to go to the Law School and be called to the Bar after all. His feeling was based on what he knew I have invested in the program both in time, efforts and money. My reaction however was that I was not looking for certificate. I am looking for knowledge. Even if the authorities decided not to issue any certificate after the completion of the 5 year course. Already I am happy with the knowledge and what I can do with it. Productive knowledge will always stand you out, with or without paper certificates.

The **third** component of the power principle is the reputation that comes by demonstration and action over time. As people see your demonstration and actions based on the reality of some sort of special power, skill, connection, networks, and the likes, they develop special confidence in you that makes them leave certain things in your hands with expectation that you will do them well. Remember the example of the man with one eye in the city where the other people are blind. His blind neighbors at certain point will start to give him respect. They will not struggle with him any longer. He now has the reputation among them that he is a better and special person among them.

Naturally, they will direct opportunities and challenges to him. Vision also helps to know that even the challenges directed to him can also be turned to opportunity. Usually, the fact that they bring their problems to you is an admission that they believe you have the capacity or ability to solve them. It is a display of their level of confidence in you. Where the confidence is properly managed it will grow to become trust. Over time, trust will grow to become loyalty. Trust and loyalty are money. They are resources that can easily give you all the money. Trust and loyalty are money in the intrinsic form. Politicians know that trust and loyalty mean money. Wise employees also know that the trust they enjoy from their employers is money in disguise. This is particularly when you are in the right work environment. The trust you earn from your fellow employees is also money in the intrinsic form. Successful businesses know that trust and loyalty enjoyed from the customer is money, It is money today and money tomorrow.

Develop or earn reputation for being able to solve problems and money has no choice than to come to you. When problems knock at peoples' door they will run to you for solution. The financially intelligent people value things that can bring money than money itself. This is particularly when that thing can bring money eventually, continually and consistently. The financially intelligent values the ability to catch and preserve fish than any amount of fish you would give them for free.

My experience in the work environment is that majority of people come alive when you have discussion about sharing money; they are actively involved when you are talking about pay, allowances or salaries. Ironically, majority of people lose interest when you talk about responsibility. They lose interest when you talk about acquiring skills or knowledge. This is why most employees don't go far in life. Even people that have been privileged to earn fat salaries at certain times in their career, they end up complaining and unsatisfied at the long run. If you have never earned fat salary before, what I just said will sound unbelievable to you. There is a very recent story of a General Manager in a Nigerian New Generation Bank. He has been on an Annual Salary of N102million (One Hundred and Two Million Naira per annum) for more than 6years. This amount excludes other allowances like medical allowance that has no limit per annum. He was advised to resign recently, only for him to start begging the employers to allow him work for an additional six months before resigning.

The natural tendency is to blame the employers for their woes, private or government. The reality is this; nobody gets far financially with an employee mentality or attitude. The employees value the salaries more than the fact that they are solving problems. And if you pay them money without adding any values they would not mind.

Being an employee is not a bad thing, particularly at certain stages of life. The real problem is living with an employee mentality or attitude to life.

BRAND AMBASSADORS

On my visit to a friend recently, I observed something. My friend's wife works with one of the telecommunication companies in town. I was also aware she had been working with the company as a contract worker. For the contract staff, the salary is usually unreasonably low. The allowances and other benefits for all other permanent staff are not usually applicable to contract employees. This contract staff are usually unhappy. They live on the hope that they would be converted to permanent employment one day.

My question that day, on whether the lady has been converted to permanent employment at last, was answered in the affirmative. However, I observed she still appeared unhappy while telling me she has been converted to permanent employment. I went on to tell her she must be rolling in big money now, considering what the telecom company is known to be paying her permanent staffs. This lady went on to tell me that the salary remains the same even after conversion. The company promised to regularize the salaries and allowances later.

She went on to express her frustration in the company's decision not to pay them as permanent staff yet. She added that the company can pay their brand ambassadors several millions of Naira, but cannot pay them, the employees well.

Apart from the fact that the ambassadors are not usually as many in number as the employees, the objective of engaging a brand ambassador is not the same as that of engaging the generality of the staff. Usually, the ambassadors are individuals who have made their reputation in their different fields of endeavour. They are usually celebrities in their different areas of endeavour. They already have their fans and loyalists. The idea is that the telecommunication company wants to leverage on the reputation of these celebrities to sell their own products and services. They want to use the celebrities to reach the fans and loyalists. In reality, the idea is that the celebrity is selling his reputation and popularity for millions of naira or dollars. The deepest reality is that the celebrity sells his or her fans to the telecom company. The celebrity would have spent a lot of resources or efforts to have millions of fans over the years.

The telecom company always conducts survey on the popularity and the number of fans a particular celebrity has before engaging them as ambassadors. The company is well aware that their fortune comes from the masses who buy their products and services. They are also aware that their success greatly depends on how many people (like the fans of the celebrities) they can get to patronize them and their services. They are therefore ready to pay heavily for any ambassador that will attract millions of fans to become their customers. The objective is either to recruit new customers, retain the existing customers or both.

The truth is that it is those customers (fans) that pay the shareholders, employees and even the brand ambassadors. And so, the company is always ready to pay any amount for their patronage and loyalty. All the ambassador does is to profit from his reputation. Good reputation can attract money in an unimaginable way.

OUTLIERS

"Success arises out of the steady accumulation of advantages. When and where you were born; what your parents did for a living and what the circumstances of your upbringing were; all make a significant difference in how well you do in the world.

The question is whether the traditions and attitudes we inherited from our forebears can play the same role. Can we learn something about why people succeed and how to make people better at what they

do by taking cultural legacies seriously? I think we can. Cultural legacies are powerful forces; they have deep roots and long lives. They persist, generations after generations, virtually intact, even as the economic and social demographic conditions that spawned them have vanished. They play so much role in directing attitudes and behavior, that we cannot make sense of our world without them." Malcolm Gladwell in his book 'The Outliers'.

No one is completely disadvantaged; each one of us has at least a combination of these circumstances to his advantage. Even in those circumstances we see as disadvantages, there are elements of benefits we can leverage together with some others for positive life achievements.

In addition, we all have inherent personal capacity to create certain advantages for ourselves. The real determinants of our lives, successes and wealth are not those advantages life bestowed on us by nature. The real determinant is the combination of how we make use of those natural advantages and our ability to create more personal advantages for ourselves.

INFLUENCE AND AFFLUENCE

This principle that makes a man to dare the seemingly impossible is the same that makes the rich individuals and corporate bodies go into projects that are almost unimaginable. Most people will find it hard to believe that many of the offices and residential facilities in Lagos Island and Victoria Island today sit on places that were once occupied by the sea water or lagoon. Even most parts of Marina/CMS were reclaimed from the sea. To attempt that kind of a thing takes specialized knowledge and resources. Many of us who did not know the time when the reclamations in the Victoria Island and Marina/CMS were done can at least see the current project at Ilubirin area of Lagos Island. The Eko Atlantic Project is another wonder piece. Governments can attempt these projects because of the power of resources available to them. They can go this far because of knowledge. There are many research results available to our decision makers which are not available to other citizens. There is a personal application to this principle. It also has corporate, societal and national application.

The good news is that any one that is willing and determined can take advantage of this principle. It is possible you already have certain powers or advantages you are not aware of. It is also possible for you to acquire specialized power or knowledge with determination, efforts and commitment. A man, with wisdom can position himself for the accumulation of necessary advantages in any area of life.

The principle dominant awareness can be summarized as follow:

1. SUBSTANCE: That is, the actual power, resources, the privilege or specialized knowledge. This has to do with the actual presence or the possession of the power, knowledge, resources, privilege or advantage. Possession of specialized power, faith, knowledge, skills, privilege or social network in a particular area affects the speed of your success in that area. Career councilors will always advise you to give priority to areas where you have some advantages when choosing a career. This principle can be applicable when it comes to money making. Today, it is very difficult to talk of success in any area without money. As far as today's world is concerned, it is even very difficult to be a successful pastor without money. A level of financial success must go with success in any other area of life. Therefore, everyone needs to be able to acquire advantages in specific areas of human endeavor. It is important to know how to translate such advantages to money equivalent. You do that by translating your known advantages to the forms that add value to human lives. When you add value to people they will pay you money in return. The easiest definition of "value add" is "problem solving".

2. AWARENESS: This is your consciousness of the unique advantage that you have which drives you to attempt what an average person around you will not attempt. The awareness breeds a unique level of confidence in you that enables you to dare what you would not naturally dare. It must also be noted that possession of advantage is not necessarily the same as the awareness of it. You can remember the story of a baby lion that grew up among sheep. That will help you to understand the difference. The lion grew up thinking she was a lamb. Lack of awareness that she possessed the strength of a lion denied her the dominion that a lion naturally commands among animals. Everyone has one or more advantage in life. Wisdom is required to search it out and put it to positive use.

That awareness makes tasks relating to that your area of advantage appear simpler than normal. One of my friends in the Polytechnic happened to be the son of one of the Chief Judges in the South Western parts of Nigeria. My friend was about two years ahead of me in the polytechnic.

He graduated with Higher National Diploma in Accountancy. He also went for the National Youth Service. To my surprise, my friend decided to go back to the University of Ilorin to start reading Law immediately after his youth service. He started a 5-year LLB Law program from 200-level. This simply means that he would spend another 4 years in the university and then go to Nigerian Law School for another one year.

He must have been brought to the consciousness of how the network and resources his father already acquired in law profession would help him to achieve success faster in the legal profession – all things being equal. Year 2001 two years into his Law Program was the year the father was retiring as a Chief Judge in the state. I was surprised to hear sometimes in 2013 that my friend has already become a Magistrate. Naturally, his rise to the position of a Magistrate was just too fast considering the practice in the Nigerian Legal environment. Normally, for any person to be appointed a magistrate, he must have at least 5 years of legal practice experience. I think my friend was appointed exactly in his fifth year in the legal practice. Whereas, there are thousands of people with multiple of decades of legal practice experience who desired the position of a Magistrate earnestly but are not appointed. The materials, facilities and network the father had built in the legal profession would have aided my friend's fast rise in the profession.

Of course, not everyone that has this kind of story have result of rising fast like my friend. What is important is to know that this is a possibility, particularly with positive consciousness of the advantage you have in a particular area of endeavour.

Not everyone whose father or mother has had a successful legal practice will also succeed in the legal profession like my friend. The amount of resources and connection such a person might have inherited notwithstanding. However, in most cases that reality and the positive awareness of it can make a lot of difference. This is particularly the reality where there are other factors to support this. Factors like the personal ability or talent of the individual and his passion along the line. All these are very important.

The consciousness of this principle is possibly one of the major factors why most prominent politicians want their children to be in politics. Most of them even want their children to get ahead in politics while the parents are still alive. This goes with the expectation that the children will have a lot to leverage on from their fathers or parents resources and social network, all things being equal. Wisdom demands that while looking for or thinking about what career or trade to invest your energy and resources in, the place where you already have advantage over others people should be the first to consider. Of course, it is possible you have an advantage in an area that is not readily noticed by everyone else. There may be gifts or talents or even passion that you have which are not readily known to outsiders and are not connected to history or inheritance. It is your solemn duty to find out such. It's also your sacred duty to show it to the world and convince the world about it. Usually, this is always a difficult task at the beginning, but with focus and commitment you can convince the world about almost anything you are so convinced of and are passionate about. When you have successfully convinced the society; that will give you the reputation on which you can rise to abundance and success.

I recently stumbled on a published content of a letter written by the then young Obafemi Awolowo while trying to solicit for a loan from Chief Adeola Odutola- then the presumed richest man in the Western Nigeria. Awolowo requested for a loan to enable him finance his trip to United Kingdom in

1943 to read Law. Chief Odutola was one of the richest men of that time.

My objective here is not to take a position on the propriety or otherwise of either the loan request by Awolowo or the refusal to give by Chief Odutola. Of interest to me is the way the young Awolowo was able to articulate his areas of strength and advantage and his determination to focus accordingly. That must have been one of the major success factors in the life of the great Obafemi Awolowo.

3. REPUTATION: This is the response of the society to the fact that you have proved to her that you have an advantage in an area of life. That advantage must result in solving certain human problem or problems. When people are so convinced you have capacity to solve their particular problem, they are ready to direct such problem to you in thousands for solution. They are also ready to pay you for solving the problem. This is a principle of life. This principle must be embraced by any man thinking of financial success. Money comes as exchange for solving problem.

Both the rich and the poor pay for solution to their problems. It is the amount they pay that differs. The truth however is that you can be rich from solving problems for any of both classes. While a few rich people can pay huge sums of money, multitudes of the poor and average people can pay small amounts that will sum up to huge fortune for you. It is important to make a choice of where you want to serve depending on your gifts, passion and area of personal advantage.

In line with the principle we have been discussing, your possession of a special advantage and the awareness of such advantage will enable you to be able to present yourself to the world for solution to problems in your area of advantage. The world in return will respond with a reputation of you in that area when you have successfully proven yourself or convinced them accordingly.

Reputation means influence. You have a place in their heart. It means you have a place in other people's thought. It means the thought of you influences their decisions. Celebrities have special places in the hearts of their fans. Therefore companies and other corporate institutions use them to secure patronage from their fans. How many people make decisions with you in their minds? What is your level of influence? There is relationship between influence and affluence most of the times.

With such reputation comes all the money. It is important to know that reputation leads to money making. And the possession of money also leads to reputation. The money you already have enables you to buy more reputation. However, there is the basic reputation that comes before such more reputation. Many of the branding efforts by successful companies and businesses are efforts geared towards buying more reputation. This is because they are aware that the society or the market pays for reputation.

I have stated earlier how big companies (telecommunication companies in this case) are ready to pay huge sums to their so called brand ambassadors as against paying their staff well. They know a good brand ambassador will make a mass impact where a staff member makes unit impact. Both the ambassadors and the staff are very important to the success of the business, but they both have different effects and impacts on the company's result.

You cannot generate a lasting wealth from a particular business until you have built lasting reputation in that area. The wise business people ensure they use the initial wealth they generate in their business to buy more reputation. **When acquired, reputation will generate more wealth for you. When sustained, reputation will generate for you sustained wealth.** The objective of this book is to saturate your mind with information that will make your actions and reactions attract money to you naturally.

THRILL OR VALUES

People don't just take buying decisions; there are usually certain motivating factors behind any decision to buy products or services. There is always a factor motivating any decision to invest time, energy and money in any particular endeavour.

Normally, the motivation for any of the decisions of buying, investing and participation and involvement should be the perceived value to be derived in such a thing or activity. Value perception is a function of many factors. Things like knowledge and exposure fundamentally influence our value perception. However, often times it goes beyond just the perceived value. At certain times people take important decisions of buying even when they cannot categorically state what value they stand to derive. You find out at certain times that certain things are done for the fun of it. Human beings are emotional beings; we are also rational beings. Human decisions are usually driven by either reason or emotion or a combination of both. Emotion and reason are two major opposing forces in humans. They are supposed to function as checks and balances against each other. Both emotion and reason are important to human life. None is good, none is bad. You cannot live a truly successful and fulfilled life without a balanced use of both.

There are people who want to run their entire lives on reasoning; they want to be rational or reasonable at all times. That is realistically not possible. It is however possible to pretend to be rational or reasonable at all times. Any sincere adult will tell you that there are a few things in life you do or say without knowing exactly why. There are decisions you take without being able to tell why you took the decisions. You may try to rationalize or justify such decision after they have been taken. Usually, we make efforts to justify where the society or the system around us demands explanation.

While it is very wrong for anyone to make most of life's important decisions based on emotion alone the truth is that we all make certain decisions based on emotion. Some of these are minor decisions of life while others are major important decisions in life. It is not unusual for you to fall in love with somebody at first sight. This is not necessarily limited to man-woman affairs. There are people you just like doing business with without knowing why at first. There are people of opposite sex that you are just comfortable having them around you. You may later make efforts to attach reasons to such unexplainable sentiments. But at the beginning you just did not know why you fall in love with such a person. It may even be a particular environment you just like or desire to work. This is usually a function of your emotion influenced by your cultivated values and exposures.

It must be stated that even though it is important to make use of our reasoning faculties when taking important decisions in life, not all emotional decisions turnout to be bad at the long run. Not all rational decisions also turn out to be good at last. Each person must learn the balanced use of his emotion and reason. It is the balanced use of both that enables us to live fulfilled lives. There are some groups of religious people who even believe that it is godliness to suppress emotion. I believe otherwise. Human emotion can be successfully controlled through the use of our reasoning ability. It can be properly guided. But truly, human emotion cannot be successfully suppressed without some negative outcome at the long run. There are ailments people suffer today simply as a result of their unnecessary efforts at suppressing their emotions. Wisdom is to know when to express emotion and when to control emotion. There are positive emotions just as there are negative emotions. Attempts to suppress our emotion entirely usually build up negative emotions at the end of the day. For example, anger, or displeasure that is not properly, rightly and timely expressed will normally aggravate to bitterness.

We cannot do a full discussion on emotion or emotional intelligence in this book; particularly as this book is not devoted to that topic. My effort here is to make you realize the huge role emotion plays in people's decision to buy your products and services or ideas. It is also to point the readers' attention to the link between emotional intelligence and financial intelligence. You must know the relationship between reputations, what people think or believe about you and their emotion. You must also know the relationship between what people think, believe or perceive about you and their willingness to pay you for goods or services.

Reputation largely rides on people's emotion. Even where people are able to rationalize why they believe whatever they believe about you at the initial stage, your real wealth comes when the majority of people fall in love with you, your services, products or ideas without probing why. It is also at this point many people decide for you simply because their friends or next door neighbors have done so. Many people just fall in love with you or your services without thinking through as to why they are doing so; they do so mostly out of conformity, In my earlier book titled 'Poverty has a Cure', we have discussed about conformity. Millions of children and adults automatically follow the steps of these so called celebrities without any scrutiny.

Majority of people want to conform because thinking or reasoning is to them a very hard job. And so they want to do what others have done or are doing; believing that the other people must have thought it through. They believe the majority cannot be wrong. Ironically, that belief or assumption is wrong most of the time. The majority has been proven wrong at many critical instances in the past. The people you are looking at to take your decision most time have also taken their own decision looking at somebody or some people somewhere.

CHALLENGING STATUS QUO

The assumption that the majority cannot be wrong is the easiest to make as humans. I think this is because we are created to live as companies, families and societies. Human beings were not created to live in isolation. This general assumption that the majority cannot always be wrong is one of the worst enemies of success and development. All major developmental strides in the history of our world have always been as a result of somebody or some people daring to have a different opinion contrary to the majority. You will do well to have a second look at the law of conformity earlier discussed in my earlier book. All Scientist in the world believed the earth was flat in shape until Galilio successfully challenged that belief. At last, he was right, all other Scientists were wrong. I believe the wrong company included his own teachers.

Most people buy certain products or services simply because they see a celebrity of their choice on the label of the product. They cannot even explain why they are in love with the so called celebrity. That is the reason most celebrities are very rich. People pay them without knowing why. That is also the reason companies use these celebrities to advertise their products. I have seen many popular Nollywood actors and actresses being used to advertize communication products, pharmaceutical products, food items and the like. Footballers and musicians are also used for different types of adverts. For God's sake, what is the connection between an actor and a pharmaceutical company or product? The truth is that there may not be a connection between pharmacy and acting or football but there is a strong connection between the actors or footballers and the pockets of their fans. Their names, pictures and voice can bring money out of their fans' pockets.

What is important to you here is to note that it is this level of reputation that guarantees wealth in any human endeavour. That reputation will not just give you money, it will give you wealth. When sustained, the reputation will also give you sustained wealth. People will not only part with their money for value they can derive from your products or services. They will also part with their money for the fun of it. They will part with their money for the thrill of doing so. When people are thrilled at parting with their money for you, your wealth is already guaranteed.

When you see politicians who have gotten to that level, they cannot be wrong in the opinion of their supporters and followers. I observed how many young people who have never met General Buhari in their entire lives were ready to die for him during the run up to the 2015 general elections in Nigeria. A number of people were reported to have trekked from Lagos to Abuja and other long distances in solidarity with Buhari even after the election.

There are thousands of people who attend even religious programs just for the thrill of seeing some popular clergies. I attended a seven day night vigil somewhere in Lagos in 2015. It was a well attended prayer programme. For anyone to attend even one-day night vigil in Lagos, it takes a lot of sacrifice and self denial. The pressure of Lagos, particularly the road traffic is one of its kind. For me, I cannot remember attending more than only one night vigil at a goal in my nine years of living in Lagos. Anyway, I had to discipline myself to attend this seven days night vigil. Thousands of people were in attendance each night. My observation was that many of the attendees were at this programme just for the thrill of it. The pastor is becoming very popular in Lagos nowadays. His name pulls crowd.

As a coincidence, there were two young ladies who sat not far away from me for four out of the seven nights. I was surprised to observe that one of them was chatting on her blackberry for more than 70% of the time at each of the meetings when we sat together. This was not a child but a full grown adult. Each time I saw her chatting on blackberry phone, I kept wondering how it is possible for an adult to deny herself sleep without an expectation compelling enough to make her concentrate on the events of the programme. The days we sat close to one another were the second to the fifth day. It was more surprising to still see the lady on the seventh day of the programme as we were filing out of the program venue. That means to me that this lady was at the program for at least five out of the seven nights of the program. It is even most likely she was around for the entire seven nights. I cannot just imagine how an adult will deny herself sleep for seven nights just for the fun or the thrill of it.

But in reality, that is the class the majority of people in any society belong. They do things just for the excitement, the thrill or the fun of doing it. They even part with hard earned money for the thrill of it. You may be surprised people eat or drink things they know are not good for their health just for the fun of it. Some even eat things that are neither sweet in the mouth nor good for the body, just for the fun of it. Most of the things done for fun soon degenerate to addiction.

Thrill is neither good nor bad. It all depends on what you do for thrill and how you arrive at doing it for thrill. Fun is neither good nor bad. It all depends on what you do for fun and how you arrive at doing it for fun. This is because maximum success in life will require that certain things in life are done for fun or thrill. That is why most personality assessments include questions about hubby or hubbies. It tells a lot about you. Everyone has the responsibility to decide what in life he wants to do for fun and the benefits he wants to derive from doing so. This decision is best taken with critical thinking and access to available information. Habits must be deliberately formed; because good habits naturally drives good success; and the drivers of habits are emotions. Therefore, you owe yourself a duty to use reason to process things very well before handing them over to emotions to drive.

I will stir up serious thoughts and questions in people if I say that addiction is neither good nor bad. It all depends on what you are addicted to and how you got to be addicted to it. It is possible to become addicted to good things just like it is possible to be addicted to bad things. Your duty is to involve critical thinking in deciding what you want to be addicted to. Emotions are also the drivers of addiction. You get addicted to a practice or something when that thing has left your thinking realm and has been unconsciously handed over to your emotion to drive.

THRILL SEEKERS

"Our culture today produces more thrill seekers." "Most individuals who enjoy the thrill of an experience try to go back and capture it without first trying to evaluate its values. Likewise, those who survive a traumatic experience usually avoid similar situations at all cost, which sometimes ties them into emotional knots."

Above are the quotes from John Maxwell's book "Thinking for a Change."

There are two major points to note from the fact that majority in our world today are "thrill seekers" or "thrill driven."

The **first** point is that people that achieve lasting success are not usually thrill seekers; they are value seekers. They are also value givers. In summary, they are value driven; and because these people are not always in the majority, not many people achieve lasting success. This is not peculiar to any society. Most societies today have thrill seekers who do things and act for the fun of it in the majority. Even when thrill seekers are able to get money at any time in their lives, they will soon throw away the money seeking more thrills. It is your duty to make conscious decision not to live by thrill but by value. That way, you continue to give value and get value in return, you are not ready to give value without getting value in return; you are not also expecting to get value without giving value back. Of course, value is very subjective. Different people attach different value to different things. Value is what we must each develop consciously. There is the value that attracts wealth; there is also the value that repels wealth. The choice is for everyone to make.

Usually, when people seek thrill for the sake of thrill, there is something they are trying to avoid. There is usually an experience the thrill seeker is trying to avoid. Sometimes it may be an experience or set of experiences he is trying not to remember. Sometimes it's a past experience he is trying to reinvent to be able to suppress the effect or prevent the occurrence of another experience. You might have heard of people indulging in the abuse of alcohol or hard drugs in an effort to avoid bad memories. They claim they want to forget their sorrows.

"We ought not to look back unless it is to derive useful lessons from past errors and for the purpose of profiting by dearly bought experience. " **George Washington.**

Before you attempt to use thrill without value as a cover to avoid a past experience; do proper analysis of the past on its own merit with a view to learning useful lessons. Before you try to reinvent a past sweet experience with thrill without value; analyze the past sweet experience on its own merit and possible effects of the past on the present and the future.

The **second** point of note is that the thrill seekers constitute a good market. For you to make your money, offer thrill to them. They will pay you even without thinking about value. Because thrill seekers are always in the majority and are always in large number, anything you sell to them will give you huge revenue. In Nigeria today, there are a number of young musicians going into production studios without any message for the public. Ironically, they come out with *noise* and you are surprised at the high level of patronage they get. A stand-up comedian recently made reference to a Nigerian musician that released an album where the only word that is comprehensible in addition to noisy beats is *banana*. The length of the album is about 16 minutes. Yet, thousands of people brought out their money to buy the album. You wonder why this is so?

While I will not advocate that you should offer thrill without value, it is important to add thrill to the value you offer. This will drive a lot of money to you over time. Thrill seekers have the habit of easily parting with their money. This is particularly when thrill is involved. They have the habit of trying to run away from critical thinking and reflective reasoning.

The point here is that you should avoid being in the company of people who seek thrill or fun at the expense of value. The second point is for you to always include them as your target market. Most of the time, they don't buy for value but for the thrill. More people buy because of packaging than because of the content. Therefore, you must always add thrill to what you want to sell. Many of the promotional activities and programmes of most big companies are targeted at this class of people. You must also note that the thrill seekers have the number. They take several decisions just once. A thrill seeker only needs to fall in love with you or your product once and thereafter he continues to remain loyal to you without thinking about it.

REFLECTIVE THINKING

Reflective thinking is required to be able to leave the crowd of ordinary thrill seekers and become a value seeker. All your decisions must be results of critical thinking and proper evaluation. You don't only think before a decision is taken, you also take time out at intervals along the line to evaluate whether the right decision was made in the first place. This analysis is not done out of fear. It is done with courage to take responsibility for decision already taken and reverse wrong decision where necessary. It is born out of commitment to value rather than out of fear of consequences of decisions already taken.

Reflective thinking is personal; it is deliberate and intentional. It is not the kind of thinking referred to as wondering thought. Even though your thoughts can wonder during reflective thinking but reflective thinking is controlled thinking. The scope of thought is very wide and open but the process is deliberate. It is organized thought. Reflective thinking is one of the secrets of great people in the world.

"Reflective thinking enables you to distance yourself from the intense emotions of particularly good or bad experiences and see them with fresh eyes. You can see with emotional maturity and examine tragedies in the light of truth" John Maxwell.

I must add that reflective thinking involves a positive attitude to life and issues of life. It goes with positive expectation based on proper analysis.

No one can possibly achieve lasting wealth without this attribute. Watch all great and transformational leaders in any generation and in any society. This attribute will be found in different dimensions in each of them.

The real cure for poverty is not in any get rich quick scheme; it can only be found in wealth building values which are cultivated and practiced consistently over time. The real cure for poverty is value that delivers wealth that last for many generations. The value we are talking about also ensures that one generation is naturally an improvement on the previous one. This is what we endeavor to teach via this book.

The first thought of writing this book came to me in 2004. I have sought information and practiced principles to test the thoughts over the years. I have published two different books after then. I have also completed work on another book which is now ready for publication. Writing eventually started in 2008. This is November 2015. It can be said that I have invested eleven years of thought and practice on the work. The work started when things were so bad that my mother had to work as a nanny, babysitter and a restaurant assistant in different places in Lagos. It was so bad she went around with my younger sister. That is, mother and daughter were employees of the same employer. I have held these thoughts and practiced the principles over the years. Even though I cannot be said to be very wealthy in terms of bank account balance today, the story of yesteryears have been completely reversed. I can also confidently say that I have left the company of the poor forever. The most important fact I must state is that I am today one of the wealthiest in the world in terms of the "wealth mentality". **In reality, when you have wealth mentality and practice wealth habits, you are already wealthy. It is just a matter of time.**

Over the years, my thoughts, attitudes and habits have also helped to transform many who came in contact with me. The result you will get from reading this book depends on you. It depends on the commitment with which you read and adopt the principles. It depends on the consistence with which you practice the principles. The principles are practiced with different levels of commitment and consistency, hence people have different results. Your result will depend on the input of commitment and consistency.

FEELING, THINKING AND ACTING

One of the greatest strength of reflective thinkers is the ability to isolate between feelings and thinking as preclude to acting. The poor and average people in life are people who find it difficult to distinguish between feeling and thinking. Ability to hold thought even when they contradict feelings is very key to financial and other successes in life. Can you feel bad and think good about a particular person at the same time? Can you identify what is good or right when it is done by that person who has currently or previously offended you? That requires a high level of emotional intelligence. There are three sides of a coin. There are three sides to a story - Your own side, my own side and the true side. Emotional, intelligence is the ability to see the truth. It is the fact that you cannot be blinded by your own side or my own side of the story.

The poor and average people are people who have always, as a matter of habit, moved from feeling to acting. This is with particular application to matters of money making, saving money and spending money. He feels like buying that item and he goes ahead to buy it simply because the money to buy it is available. He never takes time to think about the value the spending or buying will take away from him and the value it will bring back to him. He works simply because he needs money. If the need is not there, he would have no motivation to do any work. The financially intelligent are people who can work because of the natural motivation and passion to add value or ensure a particular human problem is solved. Therefore money comes as a natural bye product of getting the problem solved or adding value to other people's lives. This is one of the most difficult concepts to understand about money. Wise people apply efforts to make money. But in addition to that, their dominant thought is not applied to making money for the sake of money. Their dominant thought is applied to solving problems or creating values that will solve individual and societal problems. The focus is not usually themselves or their personal problems. The focus is the value added to others and the entire society.

This attitude to life makes all the difference between the really successful and the failures. Because of the attachment of the poor to self and personal comfort, he is so much in a hurry to get rid of discomfort that he does not think before taking any decision he feels can take away the discomfort. He does not care so much about whether such action will create for him or other people around him further problems or discomfort. He is also so attracted to personal comfort that he does not take enough time to think through before engaging in any action that promises him personal comfort. Thus the poor man is the one who usually goes from feeling to action. The rich man takes time to process his feelings through thought before taking actions in response to them. Riches here do not necessarily refer to the cash or currency that people possess at the present time. The true riches is the wealth of the mind that will lead to physical wealth in a matter of time.

The real wealth is in the values that the wealthy possess and practice. It is these values that certainly generate physical wealth over time. The story of "The Richest Man in Babylon" highlights and explains such wealth building values that when consistently practiced over time must lead to sustainable wealth building. The principles are ageless and forever remain the same. Their specific application may vary from generation to generation and one society to the other. This book's analysis of the principles from different perspectives is based on the author's expanded understanding of them. The author attempts to make it simpler than you can find in the "Richest Man in Babylon" and other books on wealth principles like, "Think and Grow Rich" and "The Science of getting rich".

I did not derive my inspiration directly from any of those ageless principle books. I came across those books and related others in the process of researching to polish my thoughts on the subject. I had read "Think and Grow rich" some years earlier before the thought of this book flashed through my mind, but did not derived the inspiration for this book directly from it.

The greatest asset of the truly rich and successful people is their thinking ability. Their greatest wealth is in their minds. Their deep thoughts gave them advantage over their peers. That enables them to see what others around them do not see. They do this by planting critical thinking between their feelings and their actions. They allow their thoughts to rule both their feelings and their actions. For the poor folks, their feelings direct everything about them. Are feelings bad? No. Feelings are parts of what makes us humans. Often times feelings are pointers to the direction our thoughts and actions must be focus. The important fact is that being controlled by feelings is living at the petty level of life. The Creator has given us the ability to think so that we can be able to develop the world we live in. Acting based on feelings will at best produce an average person or an average result.

Human beings can hardly exist without feelings. But it is possible to act without thinking. Thinking here refers to critical thinking which must be intentionally orchestrated and properly guided. The problem is that many people have not been able to distinguish between feeling and thinking. Some people think that feeling good is happiness and feeling bad is sadness. Good feeling is not necessarily the same as happiness. Think about that. Bad feeling is not necessarily the same as sadness. Ability to distinguish between good feeling and happiness and between bad feeling and sadness will produce emotional integrity or emotional intelligence in a man. You can get to the point where your happiness and sadness is not determined by feelings anymore. At that point you can determine what your feelings should be most of the time.

Any area of life you can master to this level is an area of life you can effectively control. I used to be very surprised that my grandmother felt very happy and comfortable eating things that were bitter in taste. Whereas other grandchildren and I looked for sweet things to put in our mouths, she was very comfortable eating things that were bitter. Not only that you could not see sugar in whatever form in her meal; she discouraged us from eating sugar in any form. Because I stayed long enough with her, I discovered her values around that area. My grandmother and her generation believed that substances that are friendly with the mouth (sugary items) are enemies to the body. They also believed that items that are enemies to the mouth (bitter materials) are friends to human body. They further believed that hard work and active lifestyle is very good for the human body. How they were right compared to my generation. Grandmother died at about the age of 120years without the need for much medical attention. Their generation also believed in eating from natural sources rather that eating processed items. What determined the taste in their mouth was not the items in question. What determined the taste was value they attach to the items.

Feelings are not bad in themselves. It all depends on the role we allow feelings to play in the determination of our actions.

"Any feeling that can stand up to the light of truth and can be sustained overtime has emotional integrity and is therefore worthy of your mind and heart". John Maxwell

Finally, you must note that feelings come and go but the effects of our thoughts and actions last for a life time or even long after we are gone.

Most people will rather act than think. Actions involve other physical parts of our bodies. Thinking involves the mind. The hardest work is the work that involves the use of the mind. Majority of people do a lot of things to avoid mental work. There are so many activities that are not bad in themselves except for the fact that most people use them to avoid mental work. Our comedy and home movie industry is doing great today. But millions of people spend hours before television sets or at the cinemas and shows as an escape from thinking. There are many things that can be done to generate income and wealth in any society and any generation. However, for you to generate and sustain wealth, your thought must be involved. And you require more than casual thinking. **The quality of a man's life cannot be better than the quality of his thought. Casual thinking will produce casual results. Common sense will produce common results. You cannot become great by thinking small. You cannot fly high while thinking low. Common sense will at most make a common person out of you.**

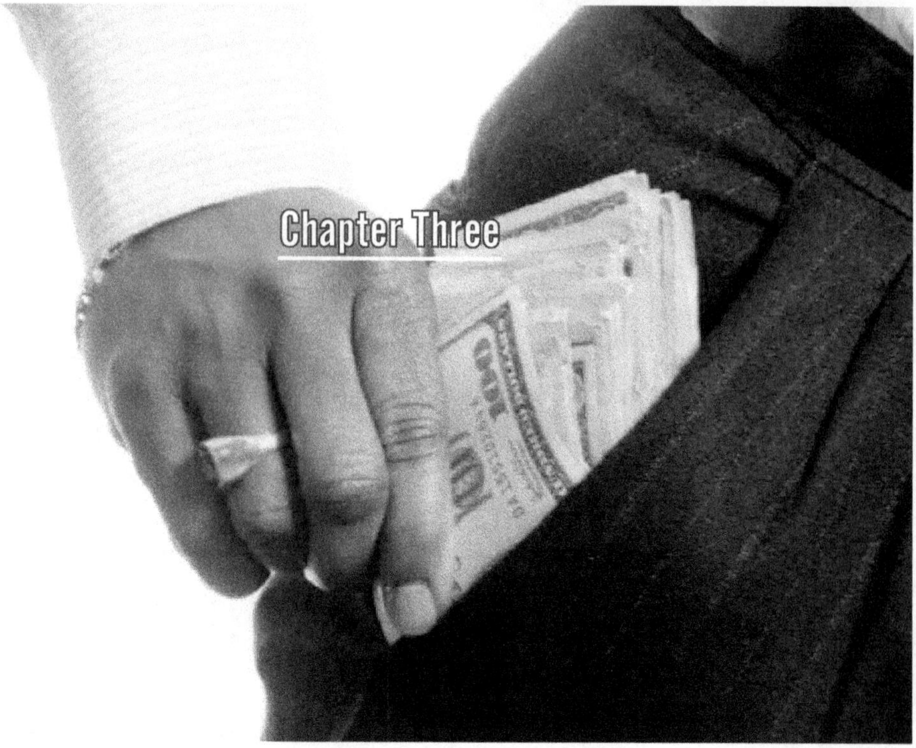

Personal Definition

LIFE DEFINITIONS

There are certain concepts that are very important to your financial life. You must have a proper perspective or definition of each of them. By definition I do not mean the definition as we used to memorize in many of our secondary school subjects. By definition we refer to your view and your dominant belief of how a particular thing should be or operate. We mean your dominant thought about a concept or an aspect of life. That thought is not necessarily what you recite. It is what is reflective in your choices and actions. It underlines your position on that concept. It underlines your attitude, behavior and habit as far as that area is concerned. Usually, these are things that appear so immaterial that an average person does not take time to think about them. But they affect the outcomes of our lives anyway. They affect us particularly in the area of success and finance.

What we do here is to highlight some of those areas where you will need to check your convictions. When you are able to establish what your convictions are with all sincerity, you can predict your financial future with mathematical accuracy. We will guide you in doing that by making you provide sincere answers to some questions. Your answers should not be provided within the orientation of someone that is trying to pass an examination. To pass an examination you do not need to state what is correct or right. You only need to say or write what the examiner expects you to say or write. The truth is you could be wrong and still pass when the examiner is wrong. You can also be right and still fail the examination. And there are many times the examiners are wrong. But they determine who is right all the same.

There was a time all the examiners believed that the earth was flat in shape. All the scientific authorities believed the world was flat in shape. At that same time, a student by name Galileo believed the earth was spherical in shape. He must have been marked wrong so many times, he might have repeated classes many times over. At the long run, Galileo was right while his examiners were wrong. During our early years in the Polytechnic, I knew some lecturers who expected a student to stay within what they wrote in their notes or handouts when answering any of their examination questions. A few of us who used to enter the library to study other authorities were marked down for not quoting within what the lecturers said verbatim. These lecturers expected students to quote exactly what they wrote in the lesson notes or the handouts. The result was that majority of the students scored high marks simply by memorizing what the lecturers said and wrote, not necessarily by understanding the principles behind the facts. I later discovered that some of the lecturers did this to encourage students patronize their handouts and handbooks authored by such lecturers. Some other lecturers also did this because they wanted to be free from doing further reading and research. And so, their marking schemes were developed from their own handout and nothing more.

In the real world, it is the principles that matters not the quotations. In the short run, it was an easy alternative for both the lecturers and students. The lecturers would not need to bother themselves with opinions and languages of other authorities on the subjects. The student in return will not be required to study wide. I was a distinction student at the time, but I saw a few other students who got grades that had no direct correlation with their levels of hard work and academic seriousness. Today we are all facing the real world. The difference is now clear. All that some of us lost in the form of marks and grades because of the laziness of many of our lecturers, we are gaining back as we are more able to confront the real life situations better. Our extra efforts were not rewarded then. Today, our extra efforts are rewarded by the results we get from the application of those principles we learnt.

Personal definitions are the expressions of principles that influence certain areas of your life. In finance and money matters, your personal definitions are so essential. They ultimately shape your life and determine your financial results. We will take a few questions to demonstrate some of them. Every one owes himself a personal duty to probe his mind concerning each of these areas. When any of these things are mentioned, what are the thoughts that come to your mind by default?

1. WHAT IS POVERTY?

There is dictionary definition of the word poverty. There is also the personal definition of poverty. There is the definition of poverty by a society. If you want to solve the problem of poverty, you must first have a clear definition of poverty. Otherwise, you would be chasing an enemy you do not know. You would be attempting to cure a sickness you don't know or have a proper diagnosis of. It is a common knowledge that solution to any problem starts by proper definition of that problem.

Unfortunately, there are thousands of people who want to overcome poverty without proper definition of poverty. To some, the definition of poverty is according to the English or French dictionary. To others, it is according to definition by the World Bank. One of the reasons why many African countries have not gotten out of mass poverty is because they use World Bank or United Nations' definition for poverty. You may draw knowledge and guidance from other people or institutions, but you must have a personal definition of the problem you want solved. You must have your own working definition.

Because poverty is a personal thing, the solution must be personal; and it starts with proper definition of the problem. Other institutions, individuals or governments can do their best to alleviate poverty for individuals or societies. But the real cure for poverty is personal. Of course, the real cause of poverty is usually personal. Other people or circumstances might influence poverty as an outcome, but the root of poverty is personal. Even where other factors have influenced the poverty outcome; the day the personal aspect of poverty is removed, the poor man has started his journey out of poverty.

There are people who are poor without knowing it, some people just assumed they are doing well financially because they are local champions among poor fellows. Such persons become either too proud or unnecessarily contented. What are the things you see in your life that are indications that you are still a poor person? No other person would provide such answer for you. It is your sole responsibility. Those things or experiences then become the symptoms of the problems you are out to solve. It is amazing how many people are poor without knowing they are poor. This is because they have not given the problem of poverty enough thought. Your business is not about poverty; it is about riches. It is not about the problem but about the solution. To that extent you don't need to be thinking about poverty; because it is what you want your life to produce that you should concentrate your thoughts on. However, since poverty is the problem, you would need to give it enough attention for you to properly define it in the first place. Defining a problem is the first step in solving such a problem.

A dictionary defined poverty as "**the state of being poor, lack of the means of providing material needs or comforts**". Another dictionary defined poverty as "**general scarcity, dearth or the state of one who lacks a certain amount of material possession or money. It is a multifaceted concept which includes social, economic and political elements.**"

The World Bank defines poverty in absolute terms. The bank defines extreme poverty **"as living on less that US$1.25 per day (PPP) and moderate poverty as less than US$2 a day. It has been estimated that in 2008, 1.4 billion people had consumption levels below US$1.25 a day and 2.7 billion lived on less than US$2 a day."**

No one gets out of poverty by just defining poverty based on dictionary or World Bank definition. You must get to a point where you know clearly what poverty means to you and what it means for you to be out of poverty. This is what majority fail to know and what makes people to go into all manners of pretence. I live in Lagos where people live their lives trying to create false impressions about their financial status. They enter into unnecessary competition with neighbours. There are people who buy cars they cannot conveniently maintain in order to create the impression that they are rich. It is common place for somebody to ride big cars (the ones people call jeep here) yet they live in houses without toilet. They buy big cars without thinking of parking space to keep the cars. There are other people who take loans to travel on vacation or go on tourism trips.

You must define what poverty or riches means to you. Proper definition must be relative. It must also apply time perspective. If you have an extended family system which you are a product of, your definition of poverty must put that into consideration. If you can live comfortably only by abandoning your siblings, you are still a poor person. I have members of my family who adopt different methods to ensure they avoid extended family responsibilities. There are others who live big but will not even pay the common security levies in the estate or street. There are others who live their lives by evading government taxes.

Yet, they want to enjoy public facilities. Some of these people are even the first to complain about failure of government. I suggest your definition of poverty must take care of all these acts of irresponsibility. If you can only be comfortable by being irresponsible, you are still a poor person. As a person and at a certain stage in life, I cannot be regarded to be out of poverty if I cannot provide support to other people in the forms of scholarship schemes to indigent students. There is a time I must be able to donate a car to someone without expecting some direct benefit from such person. At a time, I must be able to give a befitting house as a gift to another person to be able to say I am out of poverty. Of course, there is also an average financial life. Financial freedom is far beyond an average financial life. The objective of this book is not to produce an average in any one. The book is to set a foundation for any reader to come out a star over time. It is wrong for anyone to set out for an average financial life as his ultimate goal.

Take note of time perspective. If you are a secondary school student, it is enough for you to have the basic things you need for your academic program. Not owning a house cannot be included in your definition of poverty at this time, provided your parents or guardian have one that you can make use of.

Proper definition of poverty is a necessary step in resolving the problem of poverty. Proper definition of problem is the first step to a solution package. The definition is and must be personal. Don't be satisfied with being referred to as one of the masses. Don't be satisfied being called a common man or ordinary Nigerian. Each time our political leaders talk about ordinary Nigerians, my question is "who are the extra ordinary Nigerians". When they talk of the common man, I ask "where are the uncommon ones". The truth is that you know what they mean. You can also decide where you want to belong.

2. WHAT IS RICHES?

Don't continue to dwell on the definition of poverty. That is not your destination. It is the responsibility of any one that wants to be rich to define what riches means to him. What will you have in your life that you will feel that you are a rich person? What is your wealth experience like? That is, what are the experiences of your life that you will have to be able feel you are wealthy. Is this question important? Very important I must say. You must define what your poverty solution is like; that is, how your life would be without poverty. You don't get out of a problem just by defining the problem. You must go on to define the solution. And the solution must be clearly defined. With these two in place, your next important duty would be to identify specific steps of action that will take you to that solution. Then, you would need to follow the steps with dedication and commitment.

There are thousands of people out there who think they are rich while they are not. I remember a young man in Ogbomoso almost two decades ago. That was when General

Abdulsalam Abubakar's government increased workers salary, around 1998. The salary increase was as high as an average of 300%. This young teacher got almost crazy with the cash flow from his new monthly salary that was about four times of what he used to collect. He got so crazy that he had to look for married women to date. The husband of one of the women came to report him, threatening to kill him. It was in the process of trying to help him that we discovered that his problem was that he got the kind of money he never thought he could get in his life time. The problem is that he had never imagined life with such an amount of money before it actually came. He was not emotionally prepared for life at that level. So he thought that was too much money.

Have you ever imagined what it feels like to be a millionaire? What does it feel to be a billionaire? Do you imagine yourself in a position where the survival of thousands or millions of people depends on you? Think about it. You wonder why people change suddenly as soon as they find themselves in position of power and big resources? There must be something wrong to make people steal the kind of money the anti graft agencies claim they stole. In some cases, it is even beyond mere accusations because some of the accused are said to have returned such money. You wonder what they were thinking at the point of stealing such huge amounts of money. Do they even have any plan for such money?

Let me ask you this question; expecting a sincere answer. If I give you one million dollars today what will you do with it?

You think that was a simple question? The reality is that if you have never tried to ask yourself and provide some answers to these **one million dollar question**, it is not likely you would come across one million dollar in your entire life. If you ever got such money per chance, you would waste it. You will get crazy and get out of your way to do unimaginable things. That is the basic truth. It is not about the question, it is about the preparation of the mind that comes with asking and providing sincere answers to such a question.

Somebody should ask why is it that most of our forefathers in Africa were in the habits of going for a second wife as soon as they were able to build a personal house. It is most likely an indication of lack of vision. The man who built a five bedroom house could not imagine what to do with the extra rooms than to marry more wives into those rooms.

Even today, there are still some young men who cannot see any other thing to live for the moment they are able to own a car and a personal house. I know a friend whose wife will always boast among other women that 'any problem that will not cost more than money is no problem'. She boasts of how rich their family is; and in this case they don't even own a personal house yet. They cannot even afford a brand new car. Yet, she feels they are already too rich. This lack of proper definition is also one of the reasons many people in our own part of world cannot maintain and sustain wealth for a long time. Many people who were regarded as rich men and women some ten years ago are very poor today. Wealth in this part of the world hardly lasts to the next generation.

I agree with Robert Kiyosaki's definition of riches or wealth. He defines your wealth as "**the number of days, weeks, months or years you can continue to meet all your basic needs if you stop working today**". I go further to say that as long as your resources are about you and your immediate family, you cannot be said to be a rich man. I don't also see you as a rich person if your livelihood depends solely on salary, the size of the salary notwithstanding. It is important you have your personal definition of wealth. That gives you a clear goal for the medium and long term. It frees you from unhealthy competition. It frees you from a local champion mentality. It enables you to avoid waste. It places you in the league of long term thinkers. It frees you from selfishness.

3. WHAT IS GODLINESS?

There are people who think that to be godly is to be poor. Such people create religion out of poverty or create poverty out of religion. There are societies and associations that hold this erroneous belief. It is doubtful if you can remain in such an environment and become rich.

You need to change such environment. Don't only change it on the outside. Remove this poisonous idea from your internal environment. Purge your mind of this error. You must have a definition of godliness, particularly as far as money is concern. There are people who feel it is even wrong for you to be paid high for a service you have rendered, even though such payment is legitimate and as agreed upon. My objective is not to tell you which position is right or wrong. But I must tell you that this is an area that requires your conscious decision. The decision will guide your actions and choices in the pursuit of wealth and riches.

You must develop a list of your own 'non-negotiables'. That is, the list of things you cannot compromise. You must also have a list of those things you are ready to compromise. This is very important because the world of finance is full of compromises. It is a world ruled by strong interests. It requires compromise always. You need compromise as much as you need balance. Compromise is neither good nor bad. It all depends on what you are compromising and the ultimate objective of such compromise.

There are other areas of life that require compromises to thrive. Successful marriages require compromises between people of different backgrounds and orientations. Sometimes it involves people from different cultures and languages. Politics requires compromise. Business requires compromise. These are areas of life you need the acceptance and understanding of other people to succeed. They are areas you cannot succeed alone. Those other people have their own definition of godliness which may be slightly different from yours. Sometimes it is their objective that is different from yours. Learn to strike a balance. Learn to quickly identify areas you can compromise without necessarily hurting your core objective. To achieve this, you need updated knowledge and relevant exposures at all times.

When any of your position or beliefs are challenged, take time to verify your position the second time before turning down the opposing view. Many have thrown away God given opportunities in the name of religion or trying to keep established moral standards. Only to discover much later, that their positions were wrong all along. There are people who will not do business with people of other religions. That may be necessary sometimes. You must always be sure it is necessary and the best option for that moment. Always verify your belief with a view that you may be wrong in the first place. This will strengthen your position and increase your confidence in what you are doing. Unverified assumptions could be dangerous.

4. WHAT IS GOOD LIFE?

You must also have your definition of what good life is to you. What is your definition of "life well spent"? Like I have said earlier, this is more than what the dictionary says about good life. It is what you think about it. You may draw your expression from the dictionary; but the personal definition is yours. It reflects in your actions and choices and it is part of your principles. Organizations have their basic definitions. These reflect in their cultures, core values and strategic objectives.

Some people believe good life is about plenty of money. Others believe it is dangerous to have too much money. Have you met people who hold on to the belief that when you have too much money it would lead you to sin? But lack of money also leads people to sin. You owe yourself a duty to take your position ahead of time. Be conscious about it, this must go beyond what the Holy Book said about it. You can draw position from the Holy Book. But it must become your own. It must become part of your personal values. It is about the persuasion and expectation that the words of the Holy Book have generated in you. It is about the person that the words of the Holy Books have produced out of you.

These are personal decisions; your taking them will affect the outcomes of your life. Your failure to take them will equally affect the outcome of your life. There is no end to these questions. The more you ask and deliberately provide answers, the better for you.

5. WHAT IS CORRUPTION?

Corruption is one word that has gained prominence in the Nigerian national life in the recent times. By the way, there are words that have gained prominence at various times in our national life. These things come and go. Most times, the political class set the tone as to what concept dominates our national discuss from time to time. Usually, they do it for their selfish reasons making the public believe they are doing it in the interest of the public. It should not be difficult for any adult Nigerian to remember the time the word 'cabal' was in the mouth of everybody in the political space. There was a time in our history when 'colonialism' was a very prominent word. At another time it was 'independence'.

There was a time when you cannot make public speech without embellishing it with words like 'tribalism', 'favoritism' and 'nepotism'. Those were the days the ruling class made us believe that those were our problems and solving them was all we needed to enjoy good life. Those things are hardly mentioned today. I only recently discovered that the world nepotism has come back with the government of President Muhammed Buhari. Today, we have words like 'corruption' and 'marginalization'. The most recent are 'assets declaration' and 'budget padding'. Others are words like fiscal federalism, restructuring, reform, TSA, insurgence, dividends of democracy. The political class do its best to enslave the citizens with these vocabularies from time to time. Whereas, the gladiators and their motives remain unchanged.

I have followed closely the run up to the US 2016 presidential election for almost a year now; I have not heard any emphasis on the word "corruption". Are there no corrupt people in the US? There are corrupt people everywhere. The only difference is that they have passed that stage in the evolution of their national life. There will come a time in Nigeria when the word corruption will not have any prominence in our electioneering campaigns.

The truth is that it provides the political class the opportunity to run on our emotions. Today you see the very corrupt people making the loudest noise about fighting corruption. My advice to the generality of Nigerians is to be careful the way they believe politicians. Politics in this part of the world is synonymous to deception and selfishness. The word 'change' in the Nigerian Dictionary can mean just anything, depending on who is involved and the real objective you seek to achieve.

The other issue is that as a nation, we do not have a generally accepted definition of corruption. Of course, there is what our laws define as corruption. But how many of the citizens know what the laws say about corruption. That is why people's definition of corruption changes as they move up the political ladder or as they change political parties.

The point is that there are many acts of corruption that powerful people try to justify for their own selfish reason. There was a frontline politician that had been accused of many acts of corruption over the years. Surprisingly, a well respected traditional ruler came out to say that what the politician has done is "redistribution of wealth". He stated that since the man is not spending the allegedly stolen money alone, his act cannot be called stealing. We also had a president who believed that stealing is not the same as corruption. There are other legitimate businesses that people erroneously refer to as corruption. To many poor people, all the rich people are corrupt. To some other people, incorporating a Special Purpose Vehicle-SPV to do a legitimate transaction or render a service is corruption. To some people, tax avoidance is corruption.

In the light of the above, it is necessary for you to have a balanced definition of what corruption is. You need your own working definition that will guide your life, business and career conducts. This will help you to identify legitimate opportunities and take advantage of them without running foul of the laws. Always be ready to seek legal opinion where necessary. Business opinion may also be necessary. The right thing can become wrong if it is done in a wrong way. Knowledge and exposure will help. Proper documentation or lack of it can make all the difference.

GOOD LIFE PERSPECTIVES

People have different definitions of what represents good life. Whether clearly expressed or not, there is a definition of good life that shapes each person's philosophy. A society has its definition of what good life or accomplishment means. Individuals and corporate organizations in such a society work with that definition inherent in their organizational or corporate philosophies. This is well connected to the fact that our natural tendency as humans is to want to conform to the standard set by the society. This is done either consciously or unconsciously.

The point here is that your personal definition of what good life means will affect your pursuit and attainment of wealth and abundance. This is because you will naturally pursue that which you admire and definition is the expression of what you admire and desire. Your internal capacity would naturally be geared towards the achievement of that which you desire and admire. Therefore, it will be difficult for the man who assumes that rich people are bad and wicked to become rich one day. His inner resources will never be directed towards the attainment of riches. They will rather unconsciously be directed towards engendering poverty and want. The same is true of the man who believes that the rich people are the corrupt ones. This is also true of people who equate poverty, want and low -life to godliness. There are people who believe that their poverty status is instigated by God for his own divine purpose. Such people will find energy and enough excuses to remain poor.

The other side of this is the need for you to define wealth in terms of value rather than in terms of cash or bank balance. This should not be mistaken for the same thing as the belief of the people who believe that spiritual wealth is all you need. They use this as an excuse for their lack of material prosperity. My own definition of wealth is not the same as theirs. Wealth is both spiritual and physical. Both of them are important and they are not mutually exclusive. I also agree with the fact that it is possible to have material wealth while you remain spiritually bankrupt. Accumulation of material riches is by consistent practice of the principles of wealth.

Many of those principles have been taught and illustrated in this book. You can practice many of these principles with or without some critical spiritual virtues. The presence or absence of spiritual virtues will reflect or impact on your material wealth. It will reflect in what you do with your wealth. What you do with your wealth will also influence how lasting the impact your wealth will have on yourself and the society. Wealth is meant to outlive the person that accumulated it.

Napoleon Hill once defined riches or financial success in one of his celebrated teachings on wealth building. I must also recommend Hill's two books to all my sincere readers. Read his works in "Law of success" and "Think and grow rich". Ensure you read them over and over.

Napoleon Hill in his teachings "12 Things that Make Men Rich" stated what in his own definition, constitute enduring riches.

Components of enduring riches according to Napoleon Hill are listed below:

1. A Positive Mental Attitude
2. Sound Physical Health
3. Harmony In Human Relation
4. Freedom from fear
5. The Hope Of Future Achievement
6. Capacity For Applied Faith

7. Willingness To Share One's Blessing With Others
8. To Be Engaged In The Labour Of Love
9. An Open Mind On All Subjects Towards all People
10. Complete Self Discipline
11. Wisdom With Which To Understand People
12. Financial Security

The point here is that your wealth cannot be measured only on the basis of your bank balance. Lasting wealth is a total package. It is a way of life.

Chapter Four

Active Money Beliefs

MONEY BELIEFS

It has been explained earlier how beliefs are fundamental to the ultimate outcome of our lives in any area. One key area where this is very important is the area of wealth creation and retention. It must also be noted that each time we talk about wealth, we are not talking about only physical cash. There are many other things that put together with physical money will mean true definition of wealth. Money is just part of the critical resources of a wealthy person.

However, what you do with money is as important as the money itself. The importance of money is not in the figures we write or pronounce; it is about what we do with the money. The real wealth of a person is known from what he does with the money and other resources available to him. One key controller of this is the person's belief. No one can rise above his personal belief. It is the duty of everyone to be able to come to the point of believing that riches or wealth is for him. Nations of the world do not grow or develop more than the belief of the majority of people in that nation. This is particularly important with reference to the beliefs of the decision makers. It further reflects in the kind of support, acceptance and reflection the majority of the citizens and residents give to the decisions of their decision makers.

What you believe about money will ultimately reflect in and affect your ability to make money and retain it. The three fundamental areas of ability in this regard are:

1. Money Making
2. Money Saving
3. Money Spending

These are critical areas of money ability. Our capacity in each and the combination of these areas will ultimately determine who we turn out to be financially. If you want to improve your finances, be sure to improve your capacity in these three areas. Belief is however very critical to your ability in each and the combination of these areas. Our beliefs are shaped by a lot of factors as have been enumerated earlier. These beliefs end up shaping our lives, in the positive or negative.

You owe yourself the duty to take time out to verify your beliefs about money. Your beliefs will certainly be directly related to the outcomes of your financial life. There are sets of beliefs that breed poverty. There are also sets of beliefs that breed wealth. No one can carry poverty beliefs and hope to become rich. It is a principle of life. In other words, anyone that carries wealth beliefs consistently will be rich in a matter of time. The reality is that many cannot even define their own beliefs. This is because the majority of people in any society are those that are not diligent enough to take time out for a critical examination of their beliefs. It is possible to profess something whereas you believe the opposite.

If you want to know what your beliefs are, just ensure you do this exercise sincerely. Put your beliefs in the middle. See your sets of beliefs as a factory. Then see your environment, your knowledge and experience as inputs into the factory or engine of your beliefs. Also check your values and choices as the end products. The truth of what a person believes can only be established by the person's values manifesting in his choices and actions. For any poor man to change his financial status, he must first of all take specific steps to change his sets of beliefs, particularly about money.

A very handy example is the erroneous religious belief that

money is the root of all evil. There is nobody that can be rich holding this belief. Of course, there are thousands of people with some cash in their hands today, even though they hold this eroneous belief. Sincerely yours, whatever money anyone holds together with this kind of belief is the money that will soon disappear. In most of our societies, you have thousands of people who were rich in the past but today are in poverty. One of the things that could be responsible for the negative change of status is this erroneous belief. This error was preached passionately in churches in the past. It was also one of the reasons the wealth of the societies was then concentrated in the hands of non Christians.

Even as the sermon in this respect has changed in many Christian congregations, the wrong belief is still well sited in the hearts of many church people. Some clergy still hold this belief that "money is the root of all evils", even though they now preach the contrary.

Notwithstanding what you say or profess, your real belief in this regard will still manifest. For instance, there are people who belief that rich people are thieves. They just cannot believe it is possible to become wealthy without ungodly compromise. They belief you must have stolen either from government, corporate organizations or individuals to become wealthy. Again, nobody with this type of belief will ultimately become wealthy. If you are a type that gets bitter when you see rich people around, you cannot expect to become rich until you change that attitude. There are people who get angry when they see people ride expensive cars or live in expensive houses. Some try to cover up by claiming to like moderation or care for the needy people. Most of the time, all these claims are just in effort to rationalize their wrong belief.

Check the deepest parts of your heart. Do you become naturally bitter against rich people, particularly those that you are not deriving direct pecuniary benefits from? Are you always happy and feel vindicated when you hear bad news about the rich in the society. Usually, this kinds of feeling emanate from the fact that you feel inadequate by seeing the successes of other people around you. And you want to excuse yourself from blame. You get relieved when you hear that the rich also cry. Of course, there are times when some rich people in the community attract bitterness to themselves by the extravagant and arrogant way they display their wealth around many poor people in the society. The truth is that their actions are not as important as your reaction to their actions. What people say to you is not as important as what you think and say to yourself. What people think about you is not as important as what goes on in your mind. The fact that some rich people are dubious is not important to you like the fact that you believe that all the rich people are dubious. The belief that you are poor because you don't want to be dubious is a dangerous one. You have the duty to take every necessary step to change that belief.

There are people who are bitter even at people from whom

they derive direct benefits because they believe they deserve more than they are getting from such people. Most employees in Nigeria are bitter against their employers. Many people within our different extended families are bitter against their benefactors. Many people are unhappy with their relatives who are in high positions in government or corporate establishments. Many are bitter against their relatives who reside abroad. Often time we think this is just because those people are at fault. But you owe yourself the duty of taking all necessary steps to get beyond this petty level of thinking. People think this is just ordinary jealousy. This, most times is more than jealousy; it is well rooted bitterness. You must eliminate both jealousy and bitterness from your mind to create room for good ideas of wealth creation.

QUERY YOUR BELIEFS

It takes a deliberate effort for you to ascertain your real beliefs. Because of the nature of man which tends to always want to pamper himself; it is easy to assume all is well even when there are serious issues of the mind to address. As humans, we have the general tendency to over-estimate ourselves. Every man by nature works by the assumption that favours him. He easily takes the assumption and position to shift responsibility from him to other parties. He takes the position that the fault is not from him; he assumes someone else is responsible for the unpleasant outcome. At the same time he wants to take responsibility and praises for the favorable outcome. It takes a unique level of demonstration of humility and sincerity for any man to trace the cause of the problem to his or her mind. The real problem most of the time lies in the mind of each one of us. It is usually a function of our beliefs/ values, choices and actions. As far as wealth building is concerned, no one can build sustainable wealth until he learns to take responsibility for the outcome of his financial life. This is not done in the form of self condemnation or self pity. The necessary disposition is to accept the fact that you are a major factor in whatever situation you have found yourself. You must expect more from yourself than you expect from any other person. Every man is the architect of his fortune. You also need to accept the fact that the bulk in the situation lies with you. Of course, you may and usually need the assistance of other persons. But you are the most important factor. Even for you to be able to attract the kind of assistance you require from other people, your state of mind is a critical factor. The real state of a man's heart is difficult even for him to determine without a deliberate effort.

Personal examination is important. Check up your beliefs about money. Take time to find out. We all have money beliefs, right or wrong. These beliefs control the outcomes of our financial lives, just the way our beliefs in other areas of life control the outcomes of our lives in those areas. Your beliefs may be right in some areas of life while they are wrong in other areas. The results will tell. It is not unusual for you to see a man who has perfected the art of money making through the adoption of the right money beliefs, yet that same person is stocked with drug addiction. Sometimes, it is addiction to sex or any other unwholesome sexual relationship with women or men. Usually, the problem is that while such a person concentrated on the development of the right money beliefs and practices the right money habits, he has left the other important areas of life to suffer. You may have the right money beliefs and habits while at the same time your health beliefs and habits are wrong. Your money beliefs may be correct while your sex or marriage beliefs are wrong.

It is the responsibility of anyone who wants to build lasting wealth to query his money beliefs. Ask yourself critical questions that will scrutinize your beliefs, state of mind and personal assumptions about money.

What exactly do you believe about money and how do your money beliefs assist you in drawing towards your financial goals. Anybody should ask and provide a sincere personal answer to this question. It is important because majority of people work by unverified assumptions about money as handed to us by tradition. To some, it is as handed to them by their parents and grandparents. Most likely those are parents and grandparents who never had enough money to meet daily needs in their own life time. Or the beliefs and assumptions are drawn from the society of other poor people. You cannot take your most important advice from poor people. The summary of the matter is that real wealth is about the totality of who you are before it relates to what you have.

I grew up with the belief that money is only **"available in the month of a lion".** This expression is idiomatic but it tells of our people's money belief. There are thousands of my kinsmen who still hold that assumption and belief today. You cannot hold that belief and become rich. That assumption naturally conditions your mind to believe that money is very difficult to make. It is more difficult to learn how to make money than making money itself. The reason for this is that learning involves working on oneself. It involves discipline. The amount of work you will put on yourself is a function of many factors which we have so far discussed in this book. It is a function of what you already have in stock. It is a function of your environment, experience, exposure, knowledge, values and so on, which you already have in stock. With appropriate knowledge and committment, money making becomes almost autopilot.

Let me endeavor to give brief analysis about some of money (related) beliefs that may work for or against you. When you determine what you have, the next thing is to decide how to change or reinforce them as the case may be.

GOOD LIFE BELIEFS

What is your definition of good life? You need to define the kind of life you would live or where if you find another person living, you will conclude that this is a good or fulfilled life.

Look at a few examples:

1. ***Good life is about how much money you make.***

People who work with this assumption can do anything to make money. They can sacrifice anything to make money. Some can even sacrifice their lives or the lives of other people. They can sacrifice their relationships and their names. People in this class sometimes can work very hard. They work very hard for money and nothing more. When they think of money making, they do it in such a way that every other thing along the line becomes immaterial.

This belief is neither good nor bad. It is all a matter of how you hold the belief and the other things you hold around it. The problem is that people who run their lives solely on this belief get so engrossed with money making that the process with which they make the money becomes immaterial to them. They get easily crazy at the mention or sight of big amount of money. Their value most time is around making money and they forget about the important lesson of how to spend money.

The financially intelligent people know that how to make money is as important as how to save money and how to spend money. Wisdom requires you have a balanced view of all these. Without a balanced belief your values will not be properly shaped around money. Good life is more than about how much money you make. It is about how you make it, how you spend it, how you save it and how you sustain it via the right spending, saving and investing habits. It also about what impacts your money makes in other people's lives.

2. *Good life is about how much you spend.*

You must have possibly met people who boast of how much they buy some items. You hear things like **"do you know how much I bought this." "If you knew how much I bought it"?** and so on. They are people carried away with the fact that they bought certain things, particularly things that they feel other people around them cannot possibly afford. They get so carried away with the price that they forget about the value of such items. People in this category even buy things they don't need. They can steal the money they don't need in order to acquire the things they don't need. Usually, people in this class live to satisfy other people's expectation about them. And sometimes these expectations are baseless. At other times, the so called expectation is not actually set by other people; it is set by these individuals themselves for others about them. And they can do anything to meet that baseless expectation.

Good life cannot be defined solely on the basis of what or how much money you spend. Good life does not have to be expensive. There have been cases of individuals who have been opportuned to have access to huge amounts of money in life but have not been able to create equivalent value from such huge amounts of money. There have been corporate bodies and institutions that have had access to large sums of money and other resources in the past but still ended up being grounded. If you look at the statistics of companies that fail yearly, you will discover that a good number of these companies have handled money and other resources which naturally would have enabled them to survive. There are nations of the world with abundant money and other resources who are still not able to lift their citizens out of poverty.

It is not how much money you are able to spend; rather it is about how much value you are able to create by your spending decisions. Your spending of today will have direct relationship with your life tomorrow. When you understand this, you will be free from the temptation to buy what you don't really need even when you have the money to do so.

3. *Good life is about how much you give.*

This belief is very unique.This is because an average person has the propensity to be drawn towards receiving than giving. The truth is that "it is better to give than to receive." People who give cheerfully are not always in the majority. The world is full of people who receive cheerfully. This belief and level of reasoning is one of the major differences between the rich and the poor people.

Poor people feel other people are under obligation to give to them. The poor pamper and shield themselves from responsibility and obligation towards other people. The truly rich people take responsibility for other people. Most poor people are quick to accuse the rich of greed and selfishness. However, in reality, poor people are always more greedy, selfish and self centered. Sitted deep in the heart of many poor persons is selfishness without limit. Of course, there are one thousand and one ways to pretend and cover up this bad disposition. Any man that has wisely overcome selfishness is on his way to riches, all things being equal.

The greatest challenge in all this is how to create a balance between greed and selfish desire for money and legitimate accumulations of wealth for the good of many. Show me a poor man, I will show you a man that will do everything to be soft on himself and hard on other people. If you remove the effects of bad attitudes of some people who have accumulated money by accident, the real cause of the bitterness that exists between the rich and the poor in our society is deep sited selfishness. For people who are rich by accident they usually become poor again by accident; because real wealth cannot abide with selfishness for a long time. The selfish mind is usually too small to create or accommodate ideas for real wealth.

Regularly, I meet people who accuse other people of refusing to help them. One of my major reactions is to ask them how many people have they also helped or assisted in the past. The poor man sees other people as being under obligation to help him while he sees himself under obligation to help nobody. Contrary to the general belief that the rich are greedy, stingy and selfish, poor people are actually more selfish, greedy and self centered. At the root of any prolonged poverty is selfishness. Rich people give. There cannot be an enduring wealth without the habit of giving. Most poor people don't give. They rather give their poverty as an excuse.

However, it is possible to practice the act of giving out of ignorance or lack of wisdom. There is nobody who does not have at least something to give. Your duty is to give from what you have. People who believe that good life is just about how much you give usually fall into the error of attempting to give what they don't have. Good life is not about giving blindly. It is about using what you have to create better value in your life, in other people's lives and in the society around you. Habit of giving must be practiced with understanding. Otherwise, people will milk you dry.

4. *Good life is about how much you do.*

As it is with money and other resources, you only have the duty to do what you can based on the capacity and opportunity life has provided you with. Usually, there are no bases for competition. Life has not offered all of us the same opportunity. And to whom much is given much is required. When it comes to the matters of wealth creation and sustenance, the owner of a six bedroom duplex is not necessarily better than the owner of a four bedroom duplex. The man that rides a N15million car is not necessarily better than the one with a N6million car. It is all a matter of the opportunity life has provided each of us with and the value we have created out of it.

The real success in life is difficult to measure by the amount of physical things someone has accumulated without considering the type and amount of opportunity and resources life has provided that person. The story of the Bible where the Master commended the person that managed five talents well, just as He commended the person that managed ten talents provides a good guidance for us. Life is in stages and men in sizes.

5. *Good life is about me.*

There are people whose values are all around themselves to the exclusion of other people and the larger society. Each time these people think of being rich, their imagination is built around personal benefits only. They think about what they will eat and use by themselves. No one can be truly rich whose definition of riches is about himself. Real wealth is usually about how much you do for others. Landmark achievement is not possible with narrow thinking of yourself and immediate family. I gave an example of the Wright Brothers. The motivation for building the Airplane could not have been about themselves. It is only the mind that thinks in terms of solution to the problems of the larger society that can conceive such a great idea.

There was a recent publication about the discovery of a drug that can delete HIV infected cells from human systems. The scientists that made this kind of discoveries could have been on the research work for more than a decade. If this discovery is found to be true and effective, it is needless to state that the researchers on this assignment can never be poor in their lives again. It is also noteworthy that the motivations to eat food, wear clothes, ride cars and own a house could not have kept them on the research for all these years. It takes motives that are beyond just personal to achieve this type of thing.

You need to be motivated by other factors beyond just personal. That is when you can develop a heart, large enough for great achievement. Real wealth is more than being about you. According to Reverend Sam Adeyemi, **"you are too small to be the only reason for your life"**. If all you think about is about you and your immediate family, you are not likely to go far financially. The truly wealthy people are also able to see beyond today's perspective in all they do. It is not only about what you have today but also in the light of the future. That future also includes the time you would have left this part of eternity. Wisdom demands you have vision that will outlive you.

To live the life of a true achiever, you need to continually scrutinize your beliefs and your values. This is because they will both determine your choices and actions. Your financial life is a reflection of your multiple actions now and in the past.

The major work to achieve victory over poverty is on the inside. ***If you cannot think, right you cannot live right. If your thoughts improve, your life will certainly improve. If you can think better, you can live better. Work on your thoughts and your thoughts will work on every other thing that matters.***

It is necessary to remind ourselves of this because throughout the ages, the battle has always being the battle of the mind. If your mind is conquered, you are going nowhere.

6. *To be poor is to be godly.*

There are people who see poverty as a virtue. Some of them are coming from religious angle. Others are those that hold dear many of the societal values that justify poverty. These kind of belief and values will always hold down people from succeeding. You must be convinced that money is good. It is a tool in your hand. What you do with it is a matter of who you are. It is not a matter of what the money in your hand is. Money is neither good nor bad. It only takes on the character of the people that hold it.

If you believe that money is evil, you will lack passion to sincerely pursue financial goals. Without passion success is difficult to achieve in any endeavor.

7. *To be rich is to be corrupt.*

There are other people who believe rich people are the corrupt ones. I know there is a problem in our society. Deprivation and lack make many people belief that for you to be wealthy you must have stolen money either from government or private pockets. I can tell you there are millions of people who make legitimate money even in the Nigerian system. What is even most important is the impact this kind of belief will have on your drive for financial success. If you believe rich people are corrupt and evil, you will never have drive to be like them. You will also not want to learn from them. You will not be able to identify legitimate opportunity to make money.

You owe yourself a duty to deal with these issues of the mind if you will ever get rich.

Chapter Five

Wealth Puzzles

SUCCESS PUZZLE

A puzzle is like "a game, toy or problem that requires ingenuity and often persistence in solving or assembling." It involves situations that are not straight forward or are difficult to understand. It involves "a toy, problem or other contrivance designed to amuse by presenting difficulties to be solved by ingenuity or patient effort."

The world of wealth and riches is full of puzzles. The route to wealth and sustenance of wealth is not a very straight one. It amuses. It presents difficulties to be solved by ingenuity. It requires patient efforts. Sometimes it puts someone at a loss. It mystifies, confuses and baffles. Ironically, many people run on the assumption that the road to wealth is a straight one. They are wrong. That is why the same question asked a financially intelligent person can attract different answers depending on the circumstances. And yet, this is without any form of lies or deceptions. Contrary to what we learned in the school, life is more than yes or no options.

Robert Kiyosaky described wealth journey in this perspective using his teaching on the **"three sides of a coin"**. The only thing that simplifies the wealth world is that it answers to principles. It does not run on sentiment; it runs on principles. It is also devoid of extremism. It is devoid of dogmatism. What worked yesterday may not work today. In fact the opposite may be the one that works today. Usually, the principle remains the same. But application of principles changes with times and circumstance. It is the financially intelligent that thrive in this form. They are open-minded all of the time. When the relevant factors have changed, they easily adjust while still working within the principles; the non-intelligent get dogmtic and fanatical about assertions that are no longer working.

The financially intelligent are open to new knowledge on a continual basis. They don't have any permanent attachment to any habit; what is permanent is their interest. Their fundamental objectives remain stable over time. But approach and strategies change with time.

DON'T BE RIGHTEOUS OVERMUCH

About two decades ago, I came across a puzzle in my Bible. With the reputation of King Solomon of the Bible as the wisest person of his time, I was out learning from his records of wisdom. Then I was the President of my Campus Christian Fellowship of about 200 undergraduates. I learnt many fundamental wisdom principles from the records of Solomon from the books of Proverbs, Ecclesiastes and Song of Solomon. I also read from the stories of Solomon and his father from the books of Samuel, Kings and Chronicles in the Bible.

Here is the puzzle I came across one of those days. ***"Be not righteous over much; neither make thyself over wise: why shouldest thou destroy thyself? Be not over much wicked, neither be thou foolish: why shouldest thou die before thy time?"*** Ecclesiastes 7:16, 17. This quotation is from King James Version of the Bible. For the sake of clarity, let me quote from New King James Version so as to adopt its modern English. ***"Do not be overly righteous, nor be overly wise; why should you destroy yourself?" "Do not be overly wicked nor be foolish; why should you die before your time?"*** Ecclesiastes 7:16, 17.

One very important point to note in the story of Solomon is that his wisdom brought him enormous riches and wealth.

His reign as a King or President of his Nation was marked with so much prosperity and wealth. His corporate and personal life was full of affluence. He had more than his heart desired. Solomon's reign witnessed unprecedented infrastructural development. His nation enjoyed so much peace resulting from his wisdom and diplomacy. Nations around were either friendly to his nation Israel or they were subject to the nation Israel. There must be a lot to learn from Solomon by anybody who wants to build sustainable wealth and personal prosperity.

Solomon said you should not be too righteous or too wicked. He also said you should not be too wise or too foolish. What ironical combinations. What is obvious is the possibility of someone being too foolish or too wicked. Those people who are too wicked we call them "wicked". The ones who are too foolish we all call them "foolish". Is it possible to be too righteous? O yes; in this context. Can someone be too wise? Absolute yes; in this context.

From the two verses quoted above, there are so many lessons to learn. However, I have to concentrate my emphasis on the point that is relevant to this discussion. The point here is that of a warning against dogmatism, extremism and fanaticism. Even the very good things of life must be applied or done in context. My native people also believe that too much wisdom normally injures the owner of it. Because they are always able to manage their emotions properly, truly rich people are free from dogmatism and fanaticism. They are people who work based on reality drawn from available knowledge. They are committed and open to new knowledge. They are not always attached to a particular way of doing things just for the sake of it. They are committed to doing those things that work. The financially intelligent are always ready to listen to other people's opinion. They are ready to look at other peoples perspectives no matter how much their own perspective appears to be good or even the best.

There is another puzzle I found in the book of Proverbs.

"Answer not a fool according to his folly, lest thou also be like unto him. Answer a fool according to his folly lest he be wise in his own conceit." Proverbs 26: 4, 5 (KJV)

"Do not answer a fool according to his folly, lest you also be like him. Answer a fool according to his folly, lest he be wise in his own eyes". Proverbs 26: 4,5 (NKJV)

In my own words **"wisdom is to know when to speak your mind and when to mind your speech"**. The financially intelligent know how to strike a balance on all cases. They know how to properly apply their energy and available resources. Their attention and responses are always on purpose. The non-intelligent never value what they have and so proper application of it is not always important to them.

How many things can you ignore simply because they are

not important or of worthy value to your major goals at a particular time. How many events, individuals and group of people in your environment can you ignore simply because they are not relevant to your goals and objectives? Most poor people live their lives as a reaction to their environment. Rich and wealthy people live their lives as a committed pursuit of their lives' objectives. The rich avoid distractions while poor people are easily distracted.

Before I take the puzzles with which I want to illustrate the attitude of the rich, let me lay the third foundation by quoting one of the wise saying in my own part of the world.

"Little wisdom, little foolishness enjoys life." This saying appears to agree to a large extent with the two Bible quotations above. The financial world requires a balanced view. It requires ability to look at issues from different perspectives. It requires openness and readiness to learn from others, such things as may be necessary to aid our actualization of our financial and life objectives.

There are many areas of life you will need to maintain a middle course. And the financially intelligent are very good at doing that. To other average people, a one sided position is perfect. But to the financially intelligent, a one sided position can never be good enough. The one side position will come with so many disadvantages that will fully or nearly neutralize the advantages.
Let's take the puzzles one after the other.

1. Be greedy, don't be greedy

To an average mind, to be greedy is evil; he does not want to be known as greedy. He sees it as derogatory to be described as greedy. And so, he does everything possible not to be seen or called greedy. The poor are also in the habit of accusing the rich of greed. If he refuses to distribute his hard earned money to them for no just reason, he is greedy. If he does his best to make sure he gets proper rewards for his efforts, innovation and creativity, he is greedy in the eyes of his poor neighbors. The poor also finds personal consolation in being seen as someone who is not greedy. He finds that as an acceptable excuse for his state of misery and poverty. The poor man finds the best comfort in the company of his fellow poor people where they jointly form a colony of people who believe they are poor because they are not greedy and that the greedy ones are those people who live in affluence and wealth.

The reality is that there is some level of greed in everyone, rich or poor. And greed itself is neither good nor bad. The problem is the type of use we put it to. Denying the presence of some form of greed in us is denying our human nature. It is the presence of it that makes humans to be able to strive to achieve and acquire resources in life. Greed becomes evil only when it dominates your life and denies you of other human virtues.

For you to be rich, you must have a balanced view of what greed is all about. Your desire to have or acquire resources cannot on its own be evil. You must possess that desire in enough measure. You must also be proud of possessing it. Freedom from pretense is very important for true life's achievement. Many poor people who are ready to do anything just to be seen as not being greedy are mere pretenders. As a matter of fact, most poor people are actually more greedy than people who have built genuine wealth. Many poor people will steal more if only they can get access to do that. The pretense is both a disadvantage to them and to the society. I come from a society where an adult can enter into a physical fight with you if you describe him as someone who likes money. But he actually likes money, only that he is not confident enough to identify with that reality. Certain things are natural; the creator has planted a measure of them in each of us in order for us to be able to attain to the measure of His purpose for us and our world.

I have always seen male adults who accuse other men of loving or liking women. But the reality is that every male adult in his right senses likes women. To be otherwise is abnormal. Merely liking women cannot be a sin or evil. That is one of the reasons why most products and services are advertized using female pictures and female voices. The business community is aware of the fact that most economic and purchasing decisions are made by men whose decisions can be influenced by female looks and voices. It becomes evil when that emotion dominates your life and rubs you of other important human virtues. The same is applicable when it comes to man and greed. Proper understanding and application of the emotion of greed will enable you to acquire and sustain wealth within sound principles.

The advice not to be greedy cannot be complete on its own. It has to be put in perspective. You must define what is greed to you and formulate sound principles around it. Many people have missed golden opportunities to become rich just because they don't want to be seen to be greedy. Avoid that trap. Don't feel bad that you like money. You like it. That is why you spend an average of nine hours a day on your job or business. Be confident about it and be principled about it.

2. Be hardworking, don't be hardworking

Proper definition and understanding of what is hard work is very fundamental to success in life. An average person in today's society wants to be seen as hardworking. Majority have forgotten that hard work on its own does not add anything to you until it delivers the result of success or at least it moves you closer to the achievement of your goals. To many average people, hard work means efforts. And so they want to be seen to be putting efforts and nothing more. Effort without wisdom is useless. It is the wisdom content that delivers results. It is the wisdom content that delivers solution to human problems. Money follows after results manifested in the form of solution to human problems.

First, you owe yourself a duty to define what hard work means to you. I come from a society where people appreciate efforts rather than results. And so it is the prerogative of every adult to want to be seen as putting efforts in a particular thing or some things. With that, he gains some personal consolation with which he is able to justify his lack of result. Hard work is desirable but it's only desirable because of the result it produces. Any hard work that will not produce desirable results at least in the long run should be done away with. Millions of people today believe that to make more money you need to work harder. That is not always true. All that is required most of the time is to increase the wisdom content of what you do.

One basic feature of poor people is that they equate activity with productivity; this makes them to waste their energy and ability without the necessary focus on productivity. I remember how I used to think as a young boy in the village. We had some adults who were teachers and local government workers. They complained of the failure of government to settle some of their benefits and entitlements. As a boy who used to follow my parents to the farm with full awareness of how hard farming work could be, I used to assume that those office people are lazy people. My assumption was that because they were not doing the kind of manual labour that I used to do with my parents on the farm, they must be lazy. My definition of hard work was the exertion of physical energy.

If you want to be rich, you must properly define what hard work means to you. I can tell you today that I now know that mental work is harder than physical work. Although physical hard work may be necessary sometimes, physical hard work alone can never lead to wealth and abundance. Solutions to human problems over the ages have been traceable to mental hard work.

Mental hard work enables you to provide solution to human problems on a massive scale. That ability to provide solution to problems of many people at the same time is what guarantees wealth. Don't just live your live in response to the common advice to 'work hard'; 'work smart'. Don't get satisfied that you are fulfilling the moral obligation to work hard. How much money you will make and retain at the long run cannot be a function of how hard you work physically. It is a function of properly defining your financial goals and pursuing it with commitment and knowledge. Your hard work must also be properly directed.

You need to know that it is not all the time that the advice to work hard will be the solution to your money problem. Most of the time, it is not. It is even possible for you to work at your current level and become rich without working any harder. There may be thousands of people who are not working as hard as yourself but are making more money legitimately than you do. Look around, you will see them. Learn the wisdom they apply. Learn the principles; learn the skills. More importantly, learn to apply your mind more than you apply your hands.

3. Be proud, don't be proud.

This is another area where you must strike a balance if you want to live a wealthy stress free life. The general belief is that you should not be proud. Really, pride can be very bad. As a Christian, I am aware the Bible warns seriously on the danger of pride. I strongly believe that pride can be very dangerous. Many people in our contemporary time have missed golden privileges and opportunities simply because of unnecessary pride. It must also be noted that thousands of other people have also missed fantastic opportunities in their attempt to be seen as someone who is not proud. That emotion of pride is in all of us at certain measures. No one wants to be ridiculed. No one wants to be humiliated or disrespected. Everybody wants some forms of respect or even praise. I have also observed that many people who make serious efforts not to be seen as proud are actually more proud than other people. Our society is full of pretence. Acquisition of true wealth is not a friend of pretence. When you pretend, you lose the necessary impetus to pursue and defend your life's goals. You cannot excel in an endeavor you are not proud of.

Being proud becomes evil when it rubs you of other good virtues. It becomes evil when it is done at the expense of other people. It becomes a problem when you fail to have a proper evaluation of yourself. The way many of our religious organizations teach about pride and the absence of it has held many people backward. There is also the general belief that people who speak out or are naturally extroverts are proud. There are millions of people who don't speak out but are actually seriously proud and arrogant. The fact that someone is keeping quiet may even be because he is looking at other people with disrespect and disdain. Emotion of pride becomes evil when you over estimate your worth and under estimate other peoples worth.

Emotion of pride must be properly managed with knowledge. Understanding helps us to maintain a balance. Many people have remained poor because they have chosen to remain in an environment where their sense of self-worth is consistently damaged. You must apply your energy to an endeavor that you are proud of. You must consciously decide to always be in an environment that boosts your self esteem. Avoid the company of people who make you feel inadequate without opening your eyes to how to become adequate. Without a well balanced sense of self-worth and self confidence, it is practically impossible to achieve real success in life. Wise employers know that they get better results from their employees when they make the employees feel very proud of themselves. Wise parents know that they get better results from their children by making the children feel proud of themselves. They have learnt to correct or discipline the children without running down their sense of self-worth.

Political leaders get more results from their followers and their citizens when they make the citizens feel proud of themselves and of the society to which they belong.

This is one of the secrets of the greatness of the United States of America. As a nation, the United States of America has had different types of leaders in their history. However, there is an impression the US government and the citizens have managed to create. Majority of people around the world believe that US never had a bad leader. Nothing can be farther from the truth. Even though the established system in the US makes it almost impossible for any of the political leaders to perform below their minimum standards, there have been some leaders who practically implemented policies that brought the US economy backward. The prosecution of the war in Iraq is one of such examples. In spite of that, the US and its government have been able to conduct themselves over the years in such a way that the citizens and government are always proud of themselves and their nation. They feel the US is the best and greatest nation in the world.

This is unlike many of our developing countries, their citizens and leaders. As much as I admire the personality of President Muhammadu Buhari and his anti corruption posture, I have serious concern for Nigeria and her citizens when I think about the attitude of the President towards Nigerian citizens. The attitude of the president over the past months of his administration suggests that he believes that majority of Nigerians are corrupt and unholy. He stated during a debate towards the 2011 presidential election that

"Nigerians lack discipline". The president travels around the world telling them how Nigerians are corrupt people. I still believe that the bad elements among us are actually in the minority. But the President appears to travel always with messages about the corrupt minority while he forgets the messages about the good Nigerians in the majority.

Many of the statements and policy directions of the government are released when the president is outside Nigeria. Our media now quote foreign media on the position of our President and government concerning critical issues of Nigerian economy. The president talk to the Nigerian citizens using "body languages", whereas he reserves his voice and energy for western countries and their citizens whom he seems to believe have solution to all our problems. This attitude could have been proper in the era of kings and emperors who are paramount rulers of their then kingdoms. That was the era when the leaders believed they are the royalties and the citizens are the commoners.

There is this joke that is going the round nowadays, people saying that "President Buhari will visit Nigeria next Wednesday, it is not certain how long he would stay". I strongly believe the President need a lot of travels to enhance his exposure, considering that he has virtually been out of the corporate world for so long. He needs a lot of travels and interactions to be able to make up for that. At the same time, he must always do things in such a way that suggests that without Nigerians he cannot be called a

President. Customer is king. The people are the kings. There is a need for balance. We have had bad leadership at different levels in the history of our nation, but Nigerians are still better than citizens of the so called advanced countries in so many ways.

Leaders must realize the importance of leading people with their self-worth and pride intact. We can do that without necessarily justifying what is wrong. Ability to have a balanced view of two opposing world is what makes exceptional leaders. As individuals, we must all appreciate the importance of having our self-worth and pride in proper position. Don't just work by the general advice "Don't be proud", you must properly define what pride means to you. Set the limits and keep to it with understanding. Don't stay in company of people who see your effort to achieve full expression of your potentials as pride. Don't continue in the company of people who run down your self esteem. Don't follow religious beliefs which suggest that to be backward and poor is to be humble. Humility is a virtue but most of what people describe as humility in our society today have nothing to do with humility. Most times, what people describe as humility is ignorance or a combination of pride and pretence. Knowledge will help you out. Seek knowledge, you will find proper definition of pride and you will avoid it without insulting your personal sense of self worth. Seek exposure. Positive exposure will help you to achieve correct estimate of yourself and other human beings.

4. Be stingy, don't be stingy.

Being stingy is another concept whose proper understanding is very critical to achieving financial success. You will also discover that it is common place for poor people to accuse rich people around them of being stingy. Sometimes the person they are accusing is not even rich physically; he is only being prudent and responsible. Poor people are always gentle on themselves and at the same time hard on other people. I recently analyzed what percentage of my regular income goes to people in different names of charity, help and assistance.

At a time, an average of about close to 50% of my regular income goes to other people outside my immediate family. Yet, there are still so many requests I have not met.

It is good to be generous; it attracts favour both from man and from God. The truth however is that if you don't want to be named stingy in our society, it is almost impossible to be rich without stealing. You must properly work on your emotions in such a way that it runs on a balanced definition of generosity. Anything to the contrary is mere demonstration of ignorance, foolishness, and pride. You are not under obligation to solve all the problems that people present to you. Don't even attempt to do that. You are not God. It is only God that has the capacity to attend to all humans at the same time. He has the capacity to meet the problems of the whole world at the same time.

Even God works with His own divine principles. Hence, He doesn't solve all human problems. It is your duty to establish principles. Get standards; determine what you will do even before you come under pressure to do it.

You have to be ready to be called stingy sometimes. I have seen people who ask me for money while they themselves are not even ready to take any responsibility for their lives. They want to live their lives anyhow at the expense of other people. You must either avoid such people or you properly define your relationship with them. They will accuse you of being stingy; never mind them. You must always beware of people who want to set a particular standard of demonstration of affluence for you, without teaching you how to meet such unwarranted standard.

They want you to feel bad if you don't meet their expectation. Never mind them. Some of them are members of your family. Others are attached to you via some form of social relationship. Wisdom demands that you define how you want to handle your relationship with them. Otherwise, they will run you down.

Avoid every form of unhealthy competition. No one knows the type of car you should drive. No one knows the type of accommodation you should maintain. It is only you that knows what your pocket can carry at any particular time. It is not a function of whether your mates are using that type of thing; it is a function of where you are and where you want to go in life; how you want to get there and your commitment to getting there. I have seen people who don't earn half of my income and they use phones that are twice as expensive as my own. That is their choice. I would be foolish to enter into competition with them. For men who have women who like unhealthy competition as their wives; they must apply wisdom and devise a way of dealing with their wives' excesses. Without that, it will be very difficult to "get out of the valley of life" financially. Avoid the company of friends where there is unhealthy competition. Stop living your life to please people who don't matter.

5. Be selfish, don't be selfish

Possessing a balanced view about the issue of selfishness or the absence of it is critical for a successful financial life. The response of an average man is to pretend not to be selfish because of the negative impression that has been identified with selfishness over time. The truth however is that, there is an element of selfishness in every man.

Although, when selfishness is not appropriately controlled and managed, it degenerates to the point where it takes negative dimension both on the selfish person and the world around him. The selfish man can destroy just anything for his personal advantage. He can kill and do other forms of evil. All the evils in the society revolve around unguarded selfishness. Like any other emotions naturally embedded in man, selfishness could be directed to either positive or negative course. Usually, it takes the negative form when it is applied in ignorance.

The emotion of selfishness is present in everyone at some level for specific purpose which I believe is not necessarily bad. I have always used the teaching of Jesus Christ to illustrate my understanding of this matter. He said **"Love your neighbor as yourself"**. He never said you should love your neighbor more than yourself. The love for self then becomes the benchmark. That love of self is an acceptance of a level of selfishness.

Rather than condemn love for self, Christ made it the standard for loving others. There is nothing wrong in anybody having some personal interests to protect. What matters is that he must realize that other people also have interests which they are permitted to protect legitimately. Protection of your own interest must then be done in such a way that it does not amount to a direct attack on other people's interests. This requires knowledge based balanced view of selfishness.

The world of finance runs seriously on the emotions of selfishness. Most times, money made by one person is money lost by another person. Understanding gives us the right perspective which is to ensure there is an exchange of value in every financial transaction. You can actually make money without the other person losing value. There can be a win-win situation. That is, the other party has an equivalent value for the money he has to part with. Value involves some elements of perception. All you need to do is boost the value that you offer in the other person's perception. He pays you based on that perception not necessarily based only on actual value of what you exchange. Your money making is legitimate if the other party derives enough values from your offering to the extent that he is happy paying you so much.

In everything called price, there is a combination of value content and perception content. The perception component is driven by emotion. The value component is driven by solution to specific human problems.

Proper management of selfishness has been dealt with in my book "Poverty has a Cure". I also used the proverbial or comic 'Maradona' to illustrate this. You can properly, legitimately and profitably protect your interests by helping others protect their own interests. They will respond by protecting your own interest in return, in cash or in kind. You must work in the consciousness of the fact that every other person you meet is selfish. He has some personal interests to protect. Those interests may be physical or otherwise. Then, you have to respect that selfishness in people if you want to get the best from them. The recognition of selfishness in people must be from the positive point. You don't need to see their attempt to protect their own interest as evil. It cannot be evil as long as it is not forcing any other person from protecting his own interest. You can make your money or any other reward provided you do not dispossess other people of their own resources against their will. This position confers legitimacy on your money making activities.

The advice not to be selfish is good, but you must take it with caution. Everybody must have his personal definition of selfishness in the negative side of it. Putting other values of life into consideration, he must set the limits of what is acceptable to him in each case. He must define the point at which protection of personal interest becomes negative or evil. A former president of Nigeria once said his ambition does not worth the blood of any Nigerian. That is a good example of setting limit for personal interest and defining selfishness. Provided this politician really meant what he said. He must also devise the way to deal with it. This is very important because all the evils in the society have their roots in the negative emotion of selfishness. Poverty in particular is a problem that is traceable to selfishness. Ironically, poor people accuse rich people of selfishness all the time. The wise man is the one that has mastered or gained wise control over his selfishness. He is not always out to protect his personal interest alone; he is out to protect the interests of thousands or millions of other people. Those other people in response to the natural law of reciprocal will help to protect his own interests in return. You can be sure such person's interest will be over-protected at the end of the day. True wealth is derived from solving problem for other people.

If you want to be rich, you must understand the emotion of

selfishness both in your own self and in other people's lives. You must know how to manipulate this to your ultimate advantage. Take care of other people's interest first and your own interest will be taken care of automatically in return. Wealth flows naturally from protecting other people's interests simply because it guarantees the protection of your own interests in return.

6. Be Selfless, Don't Be Selfless

Our discussion on selfish emotion could have naturally addressed the issue of selflessness. Naturally, selfishness is supposed to be the opposite of selflessness. But in my own part of the world, selflessness means something bigger than the absence of selfishness. It is more than not jeopardizing the interest and welfare of other people. It involves jeopardizing and endangering your own welfare and interest for other people. I will not recommend or condemn this posture of selflessness. It can be good and it can be bad. My advice is that you live, in a world that is full of selfishness, by wisdom. You must be smart to ensure that your selflessness is not misdirected.

We are in a society where even the very selfish and self-centered people want you to be selfless towards them. This reflects in many areas of our daily lives. Let me apply this to the area of giving. People want you to give even what you don't have. I have observed over time that the demands for financial assistance I receive from family and friends are, if summed up, usually above my regular income. And each person presents his own case as if it is the law of God that you must attend to him. People do their best to make you feel guilty for turning down their demand. Ironically, these are people that have the same or better opportunities than you to make money. People want to remain lazy and irresponsible adults while you endanger your life to take care of them. Anybody that wants to accumulate wealth in our today's society must devise a way of dealing with these kinds of people around him. Define your application of selflessness in relation to this people without injuring your financial objectives. There must not be unnecessary religion about this.

I heard the story of a particular person recently which I think can illustrate this. There is one of his friends who runs to him for financial assistance. He makes a kind of distress call each time asking the friend to give him financial assistance. He has done this about three times in close succession. Because of their closeness, the friend would not naturally ask him for an explanation of what he wants to use the money for each time. Only to discover few weeks later that this friend was not actually in any distress. He had a plan to send his wife to the United States for child delivery.

You know we have many people in Nigeria who feel their children will turn out better in life if they were U.S citizens. There is no problem about that if you have the financial means. Each time this friend comes for financial assistance it was a kind of deception to get money from his friend's hand to add to the money he was trying to raise to send the wife abroad. There was no medical condition that required any procedure that could not be performed in Nigeria. At different times, this man would demand amount ranging between One Hundred Thousand Naira and Two Hundred and Fifty thousand naira. The friend would practically injure his own budget to satisfy his friend's purported need.

He was shocked to discover that his friend was actually deceiving him to raise money to send his wife for child delivery in the U.S; just for the child to be a U.S. citizen. The friend became very disappointed when he discovered that his supposed friend has actually used him to raise money for the U.S. trip. Himself could not afford such a trip for his own wife at such a time. And each time the friend came on that deceptive mission, he made this person feel that he would be offending God if he refused to grant his request for help. Ability to handle the selfishness which is the hallmark of today's society without you become selfish yourself is very important.

7. Be Careful. Don't Be Careful

The advice to be careful is a generic one. It applies to everybody and in every area of life. You are advised to be careful in business and career decisions. It is necessary to be careful in managing relationship and other important decisions of life. In general, the need to be careful in everything cannot be overemphasized. There is the need to be careful in investing and spending decisions. You have to be careful not to lose your hard earned money.

The question is whether it is possible for someone to be too careful. This is with particular reference to decisions relating to investment and money making. The general disposition in this respect is that people want to avoid risk as much as possible. However, risk and return go together. Usually, the higher the risk the higher the possible return or profit in a business. It means if you over-avoid risks, you will drive yourself away from profit.

When it comes to the advice to be careful, there must be a balanced view. It is possible to be too careful. It is also possible to be too careless. Both extremes lead to poverty. A person's view in this respect is usually a function of his natural temperament and a combination of his environment, knowledge, experience, values and beliefs. His true view is ultimately reflected in the type of choices he makes and actions he takes. It is also reflected in the failure or inability to make certain choices and take certain actions.

Millions of poor people's poverty can be traced to their carelessness. For millions of other people, the poverty can be traced to the habit of been too careful. I must add this. In my opinion, being too careful is even more dangerous sometimes than being careless. Careless people do experience some windfalls sometimes which they refer to as luck. The too careful people naturally run away from such luck altogether. The careless people always have positive expectations of life. The too careful ones are always too afraid that they often see danger in everything. The careless people usually have some measure of faith both in themselves, other people and life itself. The too careful people are usually full of doubts and suspicion. Carelessness and the habit of been too careful are too extremes that must be avoided by any person who wants to be rich in life. The two of them have the same root cause. It is the same problem that manifests in either of the two tendencies.

A medical literature I read recently explained that hypertension and diabetes are the two sides of the same coin. The two of them are traceable to malfunctioning of the heart. Even when it is influenced by other factors like life style, it is the same root problem that manifests in one person as hypertension and manifests in another person as diabetes. The difference is in other factors like individual life style, environment, eating habit and other internal factors.

In the same vein, carelessness and the habit of being too careful are different manifestations of lack of knowledge. The man with knowledge in a particular area of life cannot be subjected to fear in that area. He cannot also be careless in that area. He simply knows what to avoid. He also knows what to embrace and take advantage of. It is also possible for somebody to demonstrate confidence and courage in an area of life while he continues under the bondage of fear in another area. The difference is usually the presence or absence of knowledge. You wonder why a pilot that flies a Jumbo jet around the globe will be afraid of rats and cockroaches. A pilot is not afraid to put half a thousand people and fly them 38,000 feet above sea level across continents; yet he is afraid of blood, syringe and needle which are the easiest things for an auxiliary nurse to handle. The difference is knowledge. The day the pilot gets the knowledge of a doctor or a nurse, he will stop being afraid of needle and syringe.

If you want to be rich, you must make a personal choice to avoid carelessness and the habit of being too careful when it comes to money making. Wisdom helps you to strike a balance. That wisdom comes from the right knowledge and exposure. Many people are so afraid of investing to the extent that each time you talk of investment what they see is losses. Their consciousness of losses has so overshadowed them that they cannot even think of the returns that will come if the investment succeeds. The likelihood of failure is so real to them that they cannot even think of success as a possibility.

Rich people are those that are able to see success where others see failure. They are those that see possibility of making money where others see the certainty of losing money. Rich people are not known for avoiding risks; they take calculated risks. The calculation involves knowledge. That helps you to know what to avoid. There are many opportunities that you only need to approach them with knowledge instead of avoiding them out-rightly.

This is not a recommendation of uncontrolled greed or get rich quick syndrome; it is a call for a knowledge based response to the general advice to be careful when it comes to money matters. Good knowledge will not necessarily remove the risk embedded in your business endeavor. But it equips you with strategy to approach the risk and reduce the impacts on you when it materializes.

If you want to be careful in money matters, "be careful carefully". Good knowledge helps you to know when to follow your instinct. When you have exhausted the available knowledge at a particular time, you learn to depend on your instinct. Instinct is more powerful than knowledge. However, life is not designed to work only by instinct. You must be sure you have exhausted the knowledge available to you per time. Instinct also helps you to look for the right knowledge. Among alternatives, instincts help you to know which knowledge to embrace and to trust. The good news is that instinct is present in every one of us. Learn to listen to your inner man. Instinct helps you to take advantage of available knowledge.

8. Be Carefree, Don't Be Carefree.

Have I just advised you to be careless? No. Every one owes to himself the basic duty of being careful. The other question is whether I have just suggested you should be carefree. The answer is also no. The advice to avoid being too careful is not the same as advice to be carefree all of the time. If I have advised you to be carefree all of the time, it will be synonymous to advising you to be careless. There is no one in his right senses that will advise you to be careless. Being careless in any area of life has grave consequences that anyone must strive to avoid. After all, the choice is always yours and the full responsibility is also going to be yours.

My aunty used to boast a long time ago that she was a reckless spender. In reality, she was spending the money she did not know how the husband struggled to make it. There are other people who take pride in being carefree when it comes to money matters. It is ignorance and lack of financial intelligence that makes an adult feel good being reckless with money. It is also very difficult before you will see any one with legitimate income spending recklessly.

Reckless spending is common with people who have access to money they have not worked for. It may be a product of stealing, inheritance, gift or lottery. For people whose money comes out of efforts and financial wisdom, they cannot be carefree or reckless when it comes to money matters. They have balanced view about making money, saving or investing money and proper spending of money. Financial intelligence is about wisdom and right habit in money making, money saving and money spending.

If I advised you to be carefree about money, it is limited to you overcoming excessive emotional attachment to money in its extrinsic form. Learn to see money for what it is. It is all about exchange of value both to you and from you. I suggest you remember the story of the man that drove himself into the flame of the burning inferno of Aba International Market. He was too attached to money or resources in his store which was already engulfed by fire. He assumed there was nothing more to live for if all his life's saving was already burnt by fire. If we compare this person with Henry Ford who once boasted that if all his wealth was taken away from him in one day, he would gather much more wealth within a very short time. Henry Ford knew the real source of lasting wealth. He was also aware that as long as the source was still there, he could make much more wealth in a matter of time. The real wealth came from his mind, his intelligence demonstrated in the consistent practice of wealth habit.

You only have to be carefree as to be detached from undue emotional attachment to physical money. I have seen people who like money to the extent that they would rather keep the money in the form of a bank balance than get good medical attention for themselves or their dependants. Be carefree only to the extent that you will have the confidence to make more money as long as there is life and good health. We have heard stories of individuals who will rather drag with armed robbers at gun points than watch the money been taken away. Many people have lost their precious lives in that process.

9. Invest, Don't Invest.

It is a wise thing to invest. You need to learn to invest money, time, energy and other resources. Without investment, there cannot be return. However, an individual can get carried away with the advice to invest. The word "invest" can drive some people crazy. There are some other words that people just get emotionally attached to without wisdom. Words like profit, invest, return, risk, money, interest, love, help and so on are a few of such words. Fraudsters usually play on these words to lure their victims into misfortune. My emphasis here is on the word investing. Don't just get carried away to the extent that you can invest for investing sake. Have a balanced view of the word investing. It is not everything that is called investment that's worth your attention. There are other investments that are worthwhile but they are not for you. What is for you is a function of many factors including your knowledge, your temperament, and your available resources per time.

People come to me with attractive investment proposals every other day. A proposal can look very attractive simply because I am a novice along that line. There are people who come to me with investments that even they themselves know little or nothing about. I don't know where people get the impression that I have idle funds that I do not know what to do with it. My principle is that I don't invest in an area I do not know the basics of how it operates. I don't also mean I must have detailed knowledge of an area before I can invest in it. The basic knowledge is a must. Then how much detail knowledge I will need depends on how much I want to invest in that area. If I want to test the waters with an amount of money that does not mean so much to me, the basic knowledge will be sufficient. Otherwise, I must look for details.

Don't just get obsessed with investing, invest with wisdom. Don't also get too careful that you would rather keep your money under the pillow than invest it. Idle money depreciates fast. It is also important to know that money kept in the bank loses value, especially in an economy like ours. Bankers will always pay you below inflation rate. Keeping money in the bank serves a number of good purposes among which value appreciation is the last. Keeping money in the bank pays the bankers and the intelligent borrowers more than any savers or depositors. Safety is one major attraction of saving your money in the bank. For the society, financial Inter-mediation is another reason for saving money in the bank.

10. Diversify, Don't diversify

The traditional advice to diversify must be taken with care. The view that it is not proper to put all your eggs in the same basket sounds very normal and acceptable. Even poor people can advise you to diversify in other to be rich. The question is how come they have not become rich by their knowledge of diversification. The advice to diversify is neither good nor bad. It all depends on you. My goal is to tell you to take the advice to diversify with caution. It is not all of the time that the advice to diversify is appropriate.

I have also observed that the rich people in the world are not people that diversify. They are people that consolidate. For the rich man, he makes sure he consolidates enough in a particular area before moving to another. Consolidation in an area also means building up your knowledge base in that particular area. If you jump around, you will never be an authority in any particular area. For the rich man, moving to another area is not always a mechanism to protect him from losing the money he has already made in the initial area. It is based on passion to make more money in the new area he is going in to. Of course, there could be a time you need to reinvent your business and diversification is one of the options. Even that is a strategic practice for the rich man rather than a panic response to the fear of unknown.

Anybody that will be rich must have a proper view and understanding of this advice to diversify. The poor diversifies out of fear of losing what he already has. The rich man diversifies in expression of his confidence, courage and capacity. He diversifies because he sees further opportunities in a new area where he can make more money and express his potentials better. Rather than just diversify, the rich consolidates and expands. You can make your choice either to diversify like a rich man or diversify like a poor man.

The general advice to diversify is largely propagated by

poor people. This is one area where people make mistake of listening to the poor and hoping to become rich by implementing the advice of the poor. This is an irony. I am surprised that many of our financial experts, consultants and advisers of today are people who are poor. Many of our bankers are people who live on consumption debts perpetually. Yet, millions of people listen to their advice hoping to become rich by practicing advice propagated by these poor fellows. This is an irony. If you want to be rich you must make personal choice of whose advice you listen to. You cannot continue to listen to the poor hoping to become rich by their advice. If your advice to diversify comes from the perspective of the poor; it will only lead to poverty. The poor man's advice comes from reinforced fear.

Find out what the rich refers to as diversification; know how the rich go about diversification. It is only then you can expect to be rich like them. Warren Buffet has a completely different view about diversification compared to the thought of an average person on the street. Robert Kiosaki is also one person I know has a different view about diversification. I have also read a lot about Aliko Dangote of Nigeria. His view of diversification does not appear to be the same with that of an average person on the street.

11. Be Patient. Don't Be Patient.

The advice to be patient is another one that must be considered with wisdom. To many people, being patient is waiting for luck to shine on you one day. To others, it is waiting for God to do for you what you ought to do by yourself. Some believe patience is waiting endlessly for opportunity to come when you can create opportunity for yourself.

The rich don't just wait for opportunity; they prepare for opportunity. To them, that is what it means to be patient. To the poor, being patient is an attempt to shift the responsibility for their success to God or some other forces of nature. You must know when to keep waiting patiently and when to act. This is very important; it comes by adequate work on your mind. Don't console yourself by claiming to be patient and doing nothing. You must at all time be doing something productive. That productive effort must continue to move you closer to your ultimate goals by the day. Don't stay at home looking for job.

Ensure you take steps that daily prepares and equip you for the type of job you hope to get one day. At times it is free service you need to get involved in to prepare you for a paid job. Whatever thing you are doing at a time be grateful for that thing. That is what it means to be patient. Learn to patiently and diligently try many things until you find the one that works.

12. Be Persistent. Don't Be Persistent

Persistence is very important to any worthwhile success. However, you must be wise enough to always analyze and think through particularly when things are not working well. It is not all of the time that persistence is the key. Sometimes, failure is a pointer to the fact that you need to change your direction or your courses of action.

In summary, to be rich requires a balanced view in all areas of life that have impact on your finances. And in reality each area of your life has some amount of impact on your finances. One area might have more impact than the other. But money matter is a matter of the total man.

13. Be Contented. Don't Be Contented

Contentment is one of the basic requirements of a peaceful life. It guarantees freedom from anxiety and all its negative consequences. Contentment enables man to manage his greed properly. There is a portion of the Bible that states **"Godliness with contentment is great gain"**. To my mind, contentment that is not a product of godliness is either a manifestation of complacency or laziness. The laziness may either be of the hand or of the mind.

Majority of what people refer to as contentment have nothing to do with godliness. It has nothing to do with the fact that they want to please God. It has everything to do with the fact that they don't want to inconvenient themselves. It is a product of the attitude of "I cannot kill myself". The same people who cannot kill themselves to do legitimate things to meet their needs are the people that make unnecessary demands on other people to meet such needs on their behalf. This set of people usually don't mind if those other people kill themselves in the process of trying to help them. Selfishness and poverty are birds of the same feather. They flock together.

For anybody to gather and sustain wealth, he must have a proper understanding of the word contentment. It is foolishness to be contented with little when you can actually get more without injuring yourself or other people. Don't be contented with possessing enough just to take care of your personal needs; think broad and wide enough to be a solution to other people's problem. I have been in church services where people give wonderful testimonies of divine provision. There are people who can tell us how God granted them favor as a result of which someone else gave them a house or a car as a gift.

The reactions I see around me each time we hear such testimonies is that other people in the congregation want to believe God for such favour and testimony. They pray God will send someone to give them a car or a house gift too. There is nothing wrong in such a desire. I have also observed that each time this kind of testimony comes up my reaction is usually different. While many of the people around me were wishing and praying that they would be in the position of the person who received the gift of a house or a car, I strongly desired and prayed to be in the position of the one who gave out a house or car as a gift. I usually do that by default. I am not always contented being a receiver, I want to be a giver. You cannot be a giver and not receive in return. It is a principle of life. Even as at the time I was not able to put my children in the expensive school, I get busy daily thinking of how I can provide scholarship for some indigent children. These are not the thoughts of someone who is contented with little.

You cannot be contented with little and hope that much will come to your hand. If you are contented with little money, the best you will get is little money. If you are contented with little responsibility, the best you will get is little responsibility. If you are contented with little resources, the best you will get are little resources. For much to come to your hand becomes an accident. Usually, you would not be able to manage very well that which comes to you by accident. True success in life comes out of a combination of opportunity and preparation. Without preparation, even the best opportunity would be wasted. That is the reason you need to think wide, see wide and project wide.

There is no end to these puzzles. We can only do our best by propelling the right mindsets in people. Openness to alternatives is very important to a successful financial journey. It is important to always challenge and review the status quo.

14. Live Above Your Means. Don't Live Above Your Means

One of the most important pieces of financial advice anyone

will receive is to learn how to live below one's means.

"When people finally land a well paying job or even before that, (which is scarce), they tend to go a little overboard with buying all of the things they want simply because they can afford them now.

However, this is also why a lot of people end up with a pile of debt!

For your first couple of years in the work force, the key is to try and live below your means!

You've already had to find ways to live below your means before you landed a job, so it should be simple to continue after!

It's the best way to pay off any loans or debt you accumulated before getting your job, as well as saving up for things in the future!" Lauren Cocheane

As good as the advice to live below your means may be, no one will get wealthy only by living below his means. The real wealthy people are the ones that have learnt how to live below their means and live above their means at the same time. You must have heard about the concept of Other People's Money - OPM. Using Other People's Money is also referred to as leveraging in corporate finance. OPM is a smart way of living above your means for a positive result.

Leveraging is an acceptable way of living above your means. Therefore, the advice to live below your means must be taken cautiously.
You must learn to live below your means in the area of consumption. That is, avoid expensive living as much as possible. You must however learn to live above your means when it comes to investment and asset acquisition. This is a demonstration of financial intelligence. Wisdom is to know when to live below your means and when to live above your means. Average people believe that a coin has two sides. They talk on two sizes of a coin. They also live by that mind set. The "two sizes of a coin orientation" is conformity based. The today school system runs on that "two sizes of a coin orientation." It runs on "yes or no" orientation.

Unfortunately, the financial world does not run that way. Smart politicians also know that politics is not a "yes or no" thing. Intelligent people know that a coin actually has three sides. They know that life does not run strictly on a yes or no system. They walk with that mind set. They have broad view of issues of life, particularly financial issues.

The way up is by looking up, thinking up and acting up. You cannot go up by looking down. The balanced view will enable you to dream big and aspire high.

"I cannot emphasize strongly enough the importance of understanding the three sides of every coin, the importance of seeing things from multiple perspectives

and being open to other points of view. Parents can increase their child's intelligence by teaching them how to see a bigger picture, more than a right or wrong world." Robert Kiyosaki

"Schools are not teaching our children to be entrepreneurs. And they are crushing many dreams and demanding conformity. It's up to us, as parents, to encourage our children to believe that anything is possible, even when a schoolteacher does not agree." Robert Kiyosaki

"Live below your means." "That is actually bad advice for those with financial education. Besides, who wants to live below their means? There are too many wonderful things in life to be enjoyed. In my opinion, living below your means kills your spirit." Robert Kiyosaki

15. Be objective. Don't be objective

Being objective is when someone or his judgment is not influenced by personal feelings or opinions in considering and representing facts. It suggests the person is impartial, unbiased and unprejudiced. These are good qualities anybody will like to imbibe. Objectivity on its own is a strong sign of emotional maturity which is very important to life's achievement in any human endeavour.

Higher level of emotional intelligence is however the ability to know when to stick to your objectivity and when to allow your emotion take its course. There are instances when objectivity will no longer be a virtue. There are times you need to look away from the negatives and focus fully on the positive sides on a matter. Such instances abound in the financial world. Fault finders are not pathfinders. It took me years to be able to find out why most organizations will not promote an employee to a CEO from the position of an internal auditor. Auditors generally excel by finding faults. CEOs require the opposite disposition. The fact that someone is very critical does not suggest he will be able to deliver when given the position or opportunity.

To be a good marketer, you must learn to concentrate your energy on the good qualities of your product and play down on the defects. That is not the definition of objectivity. However, it is necessary sometimes to take such a position. This is particularly when you have a superior reason to do that. It is almost impossible to rise to the top in the world of politics if you are very objective. Politicians are known to take sides. The side to take may be good or bad. In fact, it is good just because that is the side you have taken. You are right and your opponents are wrong. That is the disposition of an average politician. To be otherwise may be an indication that partisan politics is not an area meant for you.

I have seen people who claim that they must always speak their minds. This may be a good attribute in certain instances. But there is a time this may not be necessary. There are times that being confrontational will not be the best option. Wisdom is to know when to speak your mind and when to mind your speech. You will find yourself in the situation that needs you to mind your speech in the financial world. There are times you have to align with people even though you are not totally in agreement with them. There are many times you need to keep your opinion to yourself.

16. Be independent minded. Don't be independent minded.

Independent minded people want to get things done their own way. They want to attempt to create their own solution. They want to take responsibility for the solution. They also want to get the credit most times for the success. Independent minded people break new grounds. They believe in their ability and they run with good sense of possibility. Most of the development experiences of our world are traceable to independent minded people. They don't mind being seen as the odd man out. They are goal oriented. They have fewer tendencies to want to conform to the opinion of the majority.

The Wright Brothers went on with the research and experiments even when all the scientists in America have taken a position that it was impossible to fly a machine in the air without being brought down by the forces of gravity. They were right. Independent minded people will not naturally look for the path of least resistance.

However, the route of least resistance may actually be

necessary sometimes. This is particularly when you have nothing to lose by doing so. There is no need reinventing the wheel. There are thousands who have died of sicknesses to which their next door neighbor had a solution. Independent minded people like doing things their own way. Wisdom enables you to know when to do it your own way and when to adopt the way that is already tested to be true by other people.

Some independent minded people don't work well in a team. There are times team work is very necessary. You must balance independent mindedness with team work.

Chapter Six

The Dominant Effects

DOMINANT THOUGHT

All of us are products of dominant thoughts in our minds. The dominant thoughts in our minds are also products of our environment, knowledge, experiences, beliefs, values, choices and actions.

Let me break it down further by analyzing how a man usually draws his dominant thoughts:

1. DOMINANT PERSONALITY

Each of us has at least one person whose words we hold in high esteem to the extent that his words affect the direction of our lives. That type of person is your hero. He usually goes by familiar titles like mentor, boss, parent, uncle, brother, leader, celebrity or friend. The name you adopt is not as important as the effect that person has on your life. It is important to note that each person has at least one other person that plays this type of role in his life. It is natural. Even when you have not taken time to identify who in particular plays such a role in your life; the person still exists. You may have more than one person that plays such a role in your life but, there would be one, whose words have stronger effect on you than those of other people. All of us have that natural need to draw our inspiration from someone or from a set of people.

People who have that kind of strong effect on many other people are usually referred to as opinion leaders in a particular area of life. Majority of people who hold very dear opinions that came from other people do so without raising questions about the opinion. They simply embrace the opinion as an extension of their respect for another person who holds or originated the opinion. Although, the majority of people have not taken adequate time to carefully identify where such opinions are drawn. Whether you are aware or not, you have people whose opinions shape your own opinion. Even the opinion leader has his own opinion shaped by other person's or persons' opinions. It is possible you have different individuals who shape different aspects of your life. Your belief about marriage can be shaped by one person while your belief about finances and wealth is shaped by another person.

You owe yourself the sacred duty to carefully select who your hero should be for each aspect of your life. You are not likely to be better than your hero at the end of the day. This is because your hero is a product of his own thoughts which he passes to you through his opinions. Over time, the same thoughts are reproduced in you. Overtime too, the thoughts are reflected in the relevant aspects of your life.

Look at the life of that person whose opinions you hold so sacred. Will you be happy, if your life is exactly like that in the nearest future? Then you are advised to keep it up. If not, just change your hero immediately. You cannot be listening to a mediocre and hope to come out a star. You cannot allow the opinions of poor people to rule your life and hope to become rich one day. That is why you must carefully establish relationships. Don't go into any relationship beyond casual with anybody whose life's result you don't want reproduced in you. It is also possible you admire one area of somebody's life while you detest the other area. Your first reaction is to avoid the person. If you cannot easily and readily learn those lessons you admire from someone else, then you must do extra work to avoid that aspect of his life you detest while you carefully pick those ones you admire. You should not enter into any relationship without careful consideration of the effects on the ultimate outcome of your financial life.

There are good values I cultivated from my parents. These were values of hard-work, humility, respect for human life, respect for constituted authority and so on. All these I learnt from my biological parents. However I learnt very early in my adult life that I could not learn the principles of wealth building from them. If I had just followed my parents religiously in the area of finance, I will end up in poverty without doubt. My option was to adopt those good values from them and look elsewhere for principles of wealth building. Identify your dominant personalities. Effect a change where that is necessary.

2. DOMINANT VOICE

Even when someone is not aware of who his dominant personality was, it is important for you to identify the voice you hear regularly. Whatever you hear consistently will certainly affect your life over time. The easiest indication of the dominant effect is the dominant voice. It is easier to identify the dominant voice. The voice you hear regularly will reflect in your life at the long run. It is wrong for you to absorb words without taking them serious. Whether you take it serious or not, repetition will make its effect over time. What you hear all the time will reinforce itself, dominate, shape and control your life at the long run. You can read about auto-suggestion by Napoleon Hill in his book "Law of Success".

The other important aspect of this principle is that you must consciously orchestrate some words you want to hear. Make yourself available where you will hear such words that propel you to achieving your major life's goals. Position yourself to always hear the words that reinforce your propensity towards the person you want to become in life. I continually wonder how millions of people want to be rich while they listen to poverty stories always. Millions of people want to love and be loved, yet they listen to words of hatred on daily basis. What an irony.

You also need to speak such words to yourself over and over again. If you want to be rich avoid places where they talk of poverty always. You must intentionally draw yourself towards where they talk of wealth and riches not only as a possibility but as a reality. Even when I had bosses in the office, I take time to determine whether such a boss is worthy of my attention beyond the official level. I have had a boss whose life has taught me many useful lessons about finances. I have also had another boss whose life smelt poverty all over, despite his big salary. It is my responsibility to determine the role I will allow each person's words play in my life. The types of books you read, the type of tape you listen to. The kind of film you see and the likes will have cumulative effects on your life.

The Bible also teaches all these important lessons. **'Faith comes by hearing' says the Bible; Romans 10:17. 'To him that believes, all things are impossible'; Mark 9:23. 'The**

just shall live by faith'; Romans 1:17.

The dominant voice around you will determine your faith and the effect of your faith.

3. DOMINANT THOUGHTS

Your dominant personality and dominant words or voices will work together to produce dominant thoughts in you. There are also thoughts that drop in your minds by way of imagination. They all shape the ultimate outcome of your life.

Your duty is to determine the kind of thoughts you want to allow to take root in your heart.

Thoughts are things. When you hold them long enough, they will produce their physical realities in your life. Consistent thoughts of wealth and riches will propel you to actions that will ultimately produce the physical manifestation of wealth in your life at the long run. Consistent thought of poverty and lack will equally produce its physical equivalent over time.

Every thought that is held long enough in a human heart will take root and ultimately affect the man and his environment. This is a principle of life. This has nothing to do with whether the thought is right or wrong. What matters is the presence of the thought and attention that is given to it? The presence and attention will produce faith. It is the faith that produces the ultimate results. **"If you tell a big enough lie and tell it frequently enough, it will be believed" Adolf Hitler**

4. DOMINANT CHARACTER

This is a product of your dominant thoughts. It reflects in the form of your choices and actions. It determines the ultimate outcome of your life and your future. The poor man must change his company. Because your company determines the voice you hear always. The dominant voice will determine the thought that prevail in your mind. That thought controls you to the extent of producing your dominant character. It reflects in your attitude to life.

Most great men and achievers of all generations are known to self talk. This helps them to reinforce specific thoughts or desire that affect their lives and the lives of other people around them. Self talk helps you to expel the thoughts you do not want while you reinforce the ones you want. It is usually a sign that you give enough attention to deliberate thoughts which you allow in your heart. I do not mean the kind of self talk that the mad man does along the street, but it is important you give enough attention to good thoughts in your mind. Any thought that has received enough attention in the mind will certainly come out from the month. **'From the abundance of the heart the mouth speaks'. Life and death are in the power of the tongue!**

Great people also have some level of unpredictability. This is not unconnected to the fact that their responses in life are determined by deep thoughts. This attribute enables them to see what others don't see. Their response in a particular circumstance will depend on what they see in their minds not necessarily what they see with their eyes. The same words can have different meaning. They live at the level of interest. They don't have permanent friends or permanent enemy (ies). They have permanent interests. Such interests are carefully crafted out of a rigorous thought process. The interests are continuously shaped carefully. To the great minds," it is the 'why' that determines the 'what' and the 'how' will sought out itself naturally" and not the other way round.

Chapter Seven

Six Degrees Of Financial Freedom

There is always the need to know what you are looking for. You may be lucky to meet it on your way and then your ability to recognize it becomes the most important success factor. The problem has been that majority of people talk of poverty without having the right concept of it. Millions talk about financial freedom without a clear knowledge of what financial freedom is all about. Our generation is full of many poor people pretending to be rich. They try to create a public perception that they are rich or wealthy while they are not. Of course, you can create a wealthy perception, provided you have inner resources to back it up. Overtime, the inner reality will always prevail over the external realities.

Poverty has levels. Financial freedom has levels. Wealth has levels. You owe yourself the duty to know where you are at any particular point in time. Where you want to be from time to time and your ultimate plan to getting to your financial destination are all personal questions you must answer. This is naturally not supposed to be anything peculiar. It is supposed to be a normal part of our everyday life. The problem however is that people lack the necessary knowledge and awareness about this important aspect of our lives. What the author and other trainers do is to create that awareness of the principles of wealth creation that the Creator has made as part of our universe.

To be able to drive home my point on the fact that financial freedom has levels, I have adopted one of the articles of T.D. Roth. His article points to the fact that there are different levels of financial freedom.

It shows that financial freedom is actually a journey rather than a destination. There is nothing to suggest that I agree with his analysis and definition hundred percent. But I do appreciate the way he has categorized people on the ladder of financial freedom. His analysis also supports my position on the financial freedom journey. We did not start at the same point. We don't have to arrive at the same time. The truth is that there is enough resources and time in the universe to enable each person reach his financial freedom destination. There is enough wealth in the world to go round. People should learn to collaborate and cooperate to achieve a better world, rather than competition with a view that the world's resources are not enough to go round.

T.D Roth titled his article "The Six degrees of Financial Freedom" He demonstrated how one can move from one stage of financial freedom to the other per time. I am not quoting Roth verbatim. But I will adopt his classification to draw home my explanations.

He created seven stages where six fall within the dimensions of financial freedom or financial independence as follows

"I used to believe that financial freedom meant just one thing; having enough money that you never had to work again".

"Today, I recognize there are many degrees of financial independence" said J.D Roth.

He further stated:

"Each stage of financial freedom grants you greater autonomy and self-expression and these are qualities that lead to happiness".

"Financial independence exists on a continuum. It's not "all or nothing" but an ever-increasing range of options. It's a process."

Let us look at the stages of financial freedom according to Roth.

Before you can begin to progress along the path to financial freedom, there is a preliminary hurdle you have to clear. You are in "zeroeth stage" if you don't yet earn more than you spend.

STAGE 0 – DEPENDENCE

In this stage, your lifestyle depends on others' financial support. We all start here, we're born this way. How long it takes to break free varies from person to person. You are in this stage if you rely on financial support from your parents, spouse, relatives, friends or government. You are in this stage if you spend more than you earn or if your debt payments exceeds your regular income.

It is easy to jump into conclusion that people in this stage are students and unemployed. I can tell you there are millions in our society who earn monthly salaries but are still in this zero stage. Some of them engage in businesses but they are still largely dependent on third parties for financial support. In our own society, we have them all over. I have people as family members and friends, who collects monthly salaries and yet look for excuses to collect more money from me at month ends. They present different emergencies that must be attended to. I talk to a number of people who face a similar challenge with family and friends.

Being in this stage is not necessarily a function of the size of your income. It goes beyond that. The root matter is the mindset. It also has to do with financial habit formed over time. Your choice is involved. I know a few of my family members who earn enough to take care of themselves, their immediate family and are even able to assist others who truly need assistance. Yet these people look for excuses to beg money from me and other members of the family. There are others who do everything to avoid family responsibilities, making it look like some of us who try to attend to such responsibilities do so because we have so much money that we don't know what to do with. This has nothing to do with the amount they make but everything to do with the choices they make. You can choose to be dependent or independent despite any size of income.

Since the day I left the polytechnic, I have only requested for financial assistance from my elder brother once. That was when he added about N8,000.00 for me to pay for exemption of subjects towards my examinations at the Institute of Chartered Accountant of Nigeria(ICAN); that was almost immediately after I completed my National Youth Service. In fact, I never requested for that assistance. He chose to assist me with N4000 out of the N8, 000.00 I needed to submit the exemption form. He was also the person that was going to submit the form for me in Lagos. On getting to the point of submission, payment for exemption had increased from N8,000.00 to about N12, 000.00. So he added N8, 000.00 instead of the N4,000.00 he promised me. I think he decided to do that to pacify me for turning down my previous requests for assistance. I had requested for financial support from him to furnish the apartment I secured just as I started working after youth service. My salary then was N12,000.00 per month. He had turned down that request telling me that I should learn to make do with what I had. His negative response to my request at that early stage, was part of what actually shaped my views against dependency and entitlement mentality. Rather than the national economic circumstance, entitlement mentality is the major cause of financial setback for many young people in our society today. Entitlement mentality is capable of keeping you at zero stage for a long time.

STAGE 1 – SOLVENCY

According to Roth **"Solvency is the ability to meet your financial commitments". You reach here when you no longer rely on anyone else for financial support; when your income exceeds your expenses. When you are no longer accumulating debt. When you are earning a profit, you have achieved solvency. Some people reach this stage in their teens. Some never reach it".**

This stage is like the entrance door to the financial independence dimension. How soon you will reach this stage is a function of many factors. Some of the factors are external while others are internal. Many people that are regarded as rich people in our society today are just at the solvency stage. Somebody can enter this stage either by choice or by chance. It is by chance when a number of circumstances just work in your favour for you to have good income that makes you solvent. You may be lucky to have a well-paying job, you may also come from wealthy parents. You may marry wealthy spouse or you win jackpot or lottery.

All the above and other related circumstances can work for you to be temporarily solvent. The challenge is how you maintain this position and how do you move up from here to the next level on the ladder of financial freedom. You can get here by chance but it requires specific choice for you to maintain this level or move up from here. This is the reason you have many ex-millionaires and ex-billionaires in our society. It takes a lot of hard choices to move up the ladder. Many people may not understand you. The most important thing is that you understand yourself. That understanding helps you make decisions that are not popular but are necessary for your financial stability.

I must mention this, habit of saving is one of the critical things that can take you to this stage of financial freedom.

However, saving only cannot lead to financial abundance.

STAGE 2 – STABILITY

"You achieve stability once you've repaid your consumer debt, established some emergency savings and continue to earn a personal profit. You may still possess some "good debt" - college loans and mortgage - but you have eliminated other obligations and built a buffer of savings to protect you from unfortunate events!

The issue of college loan may not practically apply in Nigeria and many other African societies. But I am sure we all know other debts that are like this. It is also possible you do not have any loan obligation. In the western societies, the fact that you are free from debt is an indication of financial stability. In many African societies this is not so. My father was very proud years back to tell me that he did not owe anybody. Yet he was a poor man. He could hardly provide us with basic comfortable living. Old theory of personal finance said you must be free from debt. New theory says you must know how to use debt to your personal advantage. There are "good debts" and there are "bad debts". My advice for you is to avoid "bad debt" abinitio.

All said, the point about movement from financial solvency to financial stability is clear. It should also be noted that for anybody to get to this point, such a person must learn prudent spending and commitment to saving habit.

However, in the today's economy, there cannot be true financial stability without stable income yielding investment. You must go beyond 'saving' to 'investing'. Value of money depreciates very fast today. It is practically impossible to become rich only by way of saving and prudent spending. There must be steady and aggressive generation of income. Your source of income must be sustainable and scalable. It must be able to respond positively to changing economic and environmental circumstances.

STAGE 3: AGENCY

"The final "Surviving" stage is free agency, the ability to work and live how and where you want. In this stage, you've eliminated all debt including student loans and mortgage and you have enough banked that you could quit your job." This is commonly called "Screw your money"

Again, the point is clear, you cannot be said to be financially free if you cannot do without a paid job. The debts referred to here are more applicable in 'credit based' societies. In a place like Nigeria, our economy is still largely 'cash based'. It is better you avoid consumer loans as much as possible. You can however use loans to your advantage in cash based society, if you have learnt how to do that. That is a different topic on its own. You may decide to buy an article on credit, even though you have cash to buy it. Parts of the ways to use credit to your advantage in a cash economy is to know how to use loan to acquire productive assets. 'Wise use of credit' helps you take advantage of inflation rather than suffer the bad side of it.

In my own philosophy, I believe you can only reach this stage when you have income from sources that are not your daily job, that are making enough to take care of your moderate lifestyle. This is achievable. You can plan for it. This book and other related materials will help you to do that.

Stages one to three above are collectively referred to as surviving stages. At this level you can be comfortable on your own but you cannot make other people rich or comfortable. Your objective must be to become a source of blessing to other people. You have to be blessed to be a source of blessing to others. You have to be rich to make other people rich.

STAGE 4 - SECURITY

"You achieve financial security when your investment income can cover your basic needs. That is, based on how much you have saved and invested; you could live a meager existence for the rest of your life. Even if you never worked another day in your life, you can have enough to afford simple housing, basic food, essential clothing and insurance".

This is the least level anybody should aspire to.

I must also add that your residual income must not be static. It must be able to respond to your changing needs. Human needs change with age. It must also be able to respond to changing factors like the effect of inflation on your income. Financial security is everyone's desire and it is achievable. Financial security is the minimum any financially intelligent person should aspire to. Financial security makes you to be able to maintain a decent lifestyle even in retirement.

The experience of the majority of people is that their standard of living is forced to drop immediately they are out of paid jobs. That is a demonstration of lack of financial security. You must learn to avoid unnecessary luxuries both before and after retirement. Asides that, there should not be a radical drop in standard of living simply because you have left paid job. This is one problem with people who get carried away with paraphernalia and privileges of high positions while in office. Free accommodation, free cars, free medicals and sometimes free food are what you must carefully and moderately handle while in service. Don't try to live the type of life you are sure not to be able to sustain when you are out of office. With good planning it is possible for you to adjust expenses pattern without sharp drop in standard of living.

STAGE 5 - INDEPENDENCE

"Financial independence is the ultimate goal for most

folks. At this stage, your investment income is sufficient to fund your current standard of living for the rest of your life. You can afford the basics, as you can some comforts too. You have enough."

At this point, you can do what you like with or without financial benefits attached to it. You can do things that give you fulfilment and impact positively on the lives of other people and the society. At this stage, your livelihood does not depend on what you make from daily or regular activities.

STAGE 6 – ABUNDANCE

"In the final stage of financial freedom, you have "enough and then some". Your passive income from all sources will not only fund your lifestyle indefinitely, but grant you the freedom to do what you want. You can share your wealth with others; you can indulge in luxury, explore the world. You can build a business empire. The more money you save, the more freedom you have and the greater risks you can take. As your financial freedom increases, you chip away at the wall of worry. You're able to make decisions based on happiness and not on dollars."

And here's the thing: As you develop smart money habits and skills, these will not only help you obtain whatever immediate level of financial freedom you're working towards, but also progress towards future levels of freedom.

If you are working towards debt freedom for instance, as you learn to spend less and earn more, this profitability will continue to help you once you've achieved solvency. You can apply the same idea as you work to obtain stability, then free agency.

DEGREES OF FINANCIAL FREEDOM

No doubt, J. D Roth has done a very wonderful work with his write up on the different stages of financial freedom. As I mentioned, we do not have to agree with everything as stated by Roth. In my opinion, his write-up will help any sincere seeker of knowledge of financial empowerment, personal money management and financial freedom mentality. It assists to systematically plan and manage one's self through different levels of financial freedom journey. I personally believe there are different levels of financial freedom from which each person can choose the one to aspire to as the ultimate objective of his financial life.

Everyone can achieve financial success or financial freedom. However, all of us do not have to achieve the same level of financial success or freedom. That will make the world a very uninteresting place because of monotony. **"Life is in stages and men in sizes."** There are many factors that may influence the stage anyone attains per time and the ultimate size of financial success achieved. For the purpose of knowledge, I want to provide some additional explanations to my readers on the categorization as adopted from J. D Roth work.

First, it must be noted that Roth was talking with significant reference to his own economic environment. That does not change the fact that he has done a wonderful job with his categorization. His explanations do not take specific notice of the dependency system in the African society. He assumes that you have all the liberty to plan and take decisions on spending, saving and investing without strong pressure from family and friends. His works assumes that you can take time to accumulate wealth and then share with people when you have attained financial abundance. In the African Society, sharing with people is not a sign that you have abundance; it is a sign that you are alive and responsible. People don't wait for you to make the money before they begin to pressurize you to spend even the amount you have not made. That is our own society for you. We also live in a society where the government fails in its own roles. It is the few responsible working class and business people that take many responsibilities which are ordinarily, supposed to be taken by the government. They are the ones that take care of the jobless and vulnerable in the society. My objective here is for you to get prepared to face serious challenge if you must build wealth and attain financial abundance in an African setting. It takes more to succeed here. But it is very possible. All you need is discipline and determination.

Another type of pressure that you should be ready to deal with is that of societal expectation. There is a way our society expects you to spend your money. There is an imaginary standard of living the society sets for you as status symbol. They make you look odd and sometimes appear foolish for not conforming to their baseless expectations. Until you are able to deal with these pressures, it will be difficult for you to get the expected result in your journey to personal financial freedom. In the American Society, it may be easy to travel the financial freedom journey as a personal one. Here in Africa, it is a journey you must force some other people to go with you or be left behind.

Some men can only travel this journey successfully after they have been able to deal with financial excesses of their wives. Sometimes, it is the man that wants to live to please the society. These are peculiarities of our own society that must be courageously dealt with before anyone can achieve financial abundance.

Secondly, I want to point to some of the important uses of Roth's analysis and categorization above.

1. It enables you reduce the journey of financial success into steps by step arrangement. One of the problems many people have is the fact that it appears very complex to move from a point of financial deprivation to point of financial abundance. It often appears impossible. That is why many wait endlessly for financial miracles. The categorization above helps you to reduce the required efforts into stages by which you can always see the current level

as a step to the next level of financial freedom.

2. It helps to be able to appreciate and determine your present status as a basis for you to set goals for the attainment of the next stage of financial freedom. We live in a society where people easily get satisfied with little of personal financial accomplishment. Many of the people that we regard as rich people in our society are people who barely can meet the basic financial needs and obligations. Many celebrated rich people in our society actually live on negative net worth. That is, when you remove all the money they owe banks and other creditors, their net assets will turn to negative.

   The problem is that our society has not properly defined what it means to be rich. Unfortunately, individuals also have refused to take that pain to develop personal definition of wealth. There are people who are still at the solvency level, yet they assume they are financially independent. Roth's categorization can assist us to sincerely determine where we are and set specific goals to get to where we desire.

3. The categorization will assist in the area of planning. It helps you to map out systematic plan towards achieving your ultimate financial objective. It makes your achievement along this line very measurable. When it comes to personal finance, many people in

our society continue at the realm of wishes. 'If wishes were horses, even beggars will ride'. My friend, wishes are never horses. Some other people move on to the level of desire. Sometimes, their desires are so strong but they are unguided or misdirected desires. Many go into obnoxious acts simply because of their strong desire and the fact that achievement of financial freedom appears to them so mysterious.

4. It also helps to demystify the achievement of financial freedom goal. It is a very difficult thing for the man who is currently suffering deprivation to be able to see financial freedom as an achievable objective. At that point, his consciousness is about lack not about abundance. His consciousness is about impossibility rather than possibility. The whole journey of financial abundance appears to him very mysterious. The major importance of categorization is to make the journey simple and the objectives achievable.

5. It makes it easy to measure progress. It is more difficult to shoot for financial abundance from a position of financial dependency. It is almost a task impossible. The categorization helps create a mental breakdown of the overall, ultimate objective of financial abundance. Any goal that is measurable will become achievable. That is the deal.

Thirdly, it is important to set financial stability as your minimum financial objective. Not everyone will end up like Richard Branson or Bill Gate. Not everyone will become like Aliko Dangote or Warren Buffet. That level of financial abundance comes with its own challenges. Not everyone is cut out for such. I am not in any way supporting the notion that some people are created to be rich while others are created to be poor. I don't believe in such. But each of us has the right to determine the type of life we want to live, after factoring in all other personal and environmental peculiarities. At the end, we cannot all end up in the same place. Whatever is your ultimate goal, you must also count the costs.

According to J. D Roth, the first three stages (Solvency, Stability and Agency) are **survival stages.** The reason is that you still need to continue to work for money if you must sustain your current lifestyle. In reality, none of us can continue to work for money for his entire life time. The law of diminishing return is an economic principle which also applies to human endeavors.

The reason why we have lots of formerly rich people in our society is because many people think they are in financial abundance whereas they are simply within these survival stages. There are people who lived in affluence when they were in active service, but suddenly became shadows of their old selves immediately they were out of service. You must have seen people who suffer different types of sicknesses immediately they are out of active service. Most times it has to do with the fact that they find it difficult to adjust their lifestyles in line with their new realities. The last three stages (Security, independence and abundance) are referred to as **thriving stages**. Therefore, the least you should aspire to is the stage of financial security.

My observations in the two different parts of Lagos I lived at different times illustrates something. In each of the cases I observed that young men who constituted nuisance were children of some so called landlords. Some of these landlords are deceased while others are still alive. Those young men grew up to become irresponsible because they were living on the assumption that their parents (fathers) were rich and there was no need for the children to be serious with life again. Looking at some of the houses the ownership of which was the basis on which these guys and their parents reached the conclusion that they were rich, you will discover they are structures that are not even befitting for human dignity. I have seen where six children inherited a six room house, one room to one person. In some cases, they have to let out such houses and you have a situation where six tenants have six landlords under the same roof. In a way, you have six governments within the six room house.

We live in a society where people simply assume or attribute the status of financial abundance to themselves or other persons simply because they could afford a second hand or fairly used car. The real problem is that people have wrong definition of what financial freedom is all about. And so, they relax too soon.

Finally, I want to add that there is no need to follow the Roth categorization dogmatically. There is no law that says you must move from solvency to stability or from stability to agency. The categorization is for the purposes of learning and analysis. Your financial journey does not have to follow line by line the way J.D Roth itemized it. In fact, you can jump stages.

The most important thing is that you must be able to reduce your ultimate financial objectives to measurable stages. You must be able to sincerely and correctly assess your status at any particular point in time. Learn to avoid being legalistic about it and at the same time take advantage of the systematic analysis the categorization has provided.

Chapter Eight

Building Wealth Momentum

EVERYTHING COUNTS

In this chapter, I itemize specific principles that must be practiced by whoever wants to become rich. They are timeless principles. The principles apply to financial success as well as success in other areas of life. Generally, people view money matters in isolation. For instance, millions of employees run with the view that success at work is a function of what you do or fail to do during the office hours.

Successful employees know that their success actually result from a combination of actions, including those ones taken outside the office. It involves the quality of thoughts you carry about your job, roles, functions, bosses and even the organization at such times while others are sleeping. I doubt whether anyone can be truly successful as an employee only by the virtue of what he does within the office hours. It has to be a complete package. It has to reflect in your entire life style and attitude. Your job must have impact on your entire life before you can expect that job to take care of your entire life. The same principle is applicable to business life.

I will deal with issues of life which majority of people view in isolation of financial success. For financial success and wealth building, everything matters. **"How you THINK is more important than how much you HAVE now to predict your future wealth." Warren Buffet**

It must be noted that the language adopted in this chapter, in some cases, are relatively lifted from ancient authors who have taught principles of success in the past. Readers may encounter expressions that are not drawn straight from modern English. Some expressions will sound like the ones I encountered reading King James Version of the Bible as a young Christian more than two decades ago. The principles itemized on the following pages are literal summary of the wealth building principles that have been taught over the previous chapters of this book. Any reader will do himself the best of good by paying necessary attention.

I have adopted the narrative approach in the most parts of the book so far. In this chapter and the next, the approach will be a little different. It may look more like speech writing. The idea is to use this approach to provide literal summary of the principles already taught using narrative approach so far. This reduces the principles to specific points which readers can easily remember.

I have quoted from the works of people like Wallace D. Wattles, Napoleon Hill, Andrew Carnegie, McGrew Hill and others. Most of their materials came into circulation between 1880 and 1940. They are currently in the public domain. Readers are advised to study further the thoughts from these great minds. You will do well to read through their works like "The Science of Getting Rich" by Wallace D. Wattles, "The Science of Being Great" by Wallace D. Wattles, "Gospel of Wealth" by Andrew Carnegie, "Think and Grow Rich" by Napoleon Hill, "Law of Success Course" by Napoleon Hill and "The Law of Financial Success" by McGrew Hill among others.

UNIVERSAL LAWS

Is there really a fundamental law underlying that which we call financial success? Is there a law which if once discovered, understood and practiced well, will make one the master of financial success. Is indeed financial success the result of the operation of a law, instead of the operation of mere luck, chances or accidents?

Absolute yes; all the money we seek comes only from the application and operation of a great law which the successful men and women of the world make use of either consciously or unconsciously. And this great law is as well defined as any other natural law; and when grasped and understood may be practiced and operated just as any of its related laws on other planes of human endeavours.

"There is no such thing in nature as blind chances, accidents or uncaused luck. Everything in nature operates in accordance with laws. Law underlies everything; there is nothing in our finite world that is not the effect of some cause.

Man can make a servant and a slave of a universal law, instead of allowing it to master him and become his tyrant. This is the way he has mastered the forces of gravitation (gravity), steam, hydraulics and electricity which once mastered man.

Ray Lankester said: "**Man is held to be a part of Nature, a product of the definite and orderly evolution which is universal, a being resulting from and driven by the one great nexus of mechanism which we call Nature. He stands alone, face to face with the relentless mechanism. It is his destiny to understand and control it.**" All progress whether physical, mental, moral, spiritual or financial is based upon law. And he who wins success in any line does so because he has followed the law or laws pertaining to his business, whether he does it consciously or unconsciously.

Some of our great business men and captains of industry who have won marvelous success in financial affairs (though they may have failed as moral spiritual beings), have won their great successes along this line because they have discovered the underlying law and by concentrating upon it alone, to the exclusion of everything else in life, have mastered the operation of the law to an almost abnormal degree. This they might have done consciously or unconsciously."

Discovery and application of the law requires personal decision and conscious efforts.

POINTS OF VIEW AND MONEY DESIRE

There is so much misconception of the idea of money. On one hand we find many engaged in a mad chase after money for money's sake. On the other hand; there are many other people who are decrying money as the root of all evil, and severely criticizing the tendency of the age to seek money actively. Both of these classes of people are wrong - they are occupying the opposite side of the road of reason.

People who worship money as god are mistaking the symbol for the reality. Likewise, the man who decries the pursuit and desire for money as a foul evil thus is a fool.

Wisdom is to see money as a symbol of something else behind, and not being deluded by mistaking the shadow for the substances, either for good or for evil. The wise man makes neither a god nor a devil of money. Almost everything that man may obtain from the outside world for his development and fulfillment requires the use of money. While it is true that selfishness and greed are detestable status of mind, still the lack of the proper desire for and striving after money, makes of a man a creature devoid of all that makes life worth the living.

Money is but the concentrated essence of things desired, created and established by society in its present stage of development. There have been times in which there was no money; there may be times coming in which the human race will have passed beyond the need of money as the symbol of exchange and possession. For now, within the first quarter of twenty-first century, possession of money is a major part of the definition of success.

In summary, when we say man needs the many things that money will purchase for him we mean that he needs the values that come with the many things that money will purchase for him. Money means freedom, independence, liberty and the ability to do great good as well as great evil. It means opportunity to carry out your legitimate desires.

I hold that in the present stage of evolution of man, money is to mankind what air, water, sunshine and mother-earth are to plant. It is nourishment. And, as in the plant, the desire for nourishment is a natural and worthy instinct, so is the desire for this financial nourishment in a man perfectly natural and worthy instinct. It involves the working of the same natural law. Also, as the desire for nourishment by plant is a natural indication of the existence of the nourishment needed, so is this desire in the breast of man a certain indication of the possibility of its satisfaction and attainment. Nature is no mocker - it causes no desire to spring up in a living thing without facilitation and powers to attain that which it craves. A realization of this great natural laws will do us much good.

Stop all the talk of the beauty of poverty and the joy of the humble. Throw off this mask of hypocrisy and self-deception and stand out in the open like a man, throw your head up and look the world in the face, say " yes I do desire money" desire it and make legitimate demand for it. This is a very critical step towards accumulation of money.

MENTAL ATTITUDE

One's place in life is largely determined by his mental attitude. Mental attitude is the result of the currency of one's thoughts, ideas, ideals, feelings and beliefs. You are constantly at work building up a mental attitude, which is not only making your character but which is also having its effects upon the outside world both in the direction of your influence upon other people, as well as your quality of attracting towards yourself that which is in agreement with your strongest inner desires.

A positive mental attitude wins financial success. Positive means confident expectation, self-confidence, courage, initiative, energy, optimism, expectations of good not of evil - of wealth, not of poverty - believe in oneself and in the natural law of success. Negative means fear, worry, expectation of undesirable things and lack of confidence in oneself and natural law of success.

There are great scientific authorities in support of the fact that by diligent care and practice, one may completely change his character, temperament and habits. He may eliminate undesirable traits of character and replace them by new desirable traits, qualities and faculties.

Prevailing mental attitude is the pattern upon which the brain cells build.

The brain is known to be the instrument and tool of the mind, the mind uses the brain as an instrument of expression. Also, the brain is known to be made up of millions of tiny cells, majority of which are not in use. Hence, if one turns his attention and interest in certain directions, the unused cells in the area of his brain which is the center of such subject will be stimulated into action and will begin to manifest actively. The stimulated sections of cells will begin also to actively manifest the reproductive qualities, and new brain cells will be evolved, grown and developed in order to furnish proper mental tools with which tools to manifest the new desires, qualities and feelings pressing forward for expression. This is the same process with which addictions are formed. It relates to both positive and negative addiction the same way.

SUGGESTIVE IMPRESSION

Next to this is the fact that your mental attitude reflects and gives people around and in contact with you suggestive impression of yourself and your qualities. They form impression and conduct themselves, towards you accordingly.

A man full of positive thoughts, feelings and ideas of enthusiasm, success, self-confidence, confidence in his proposition and objective will always radiate success. Other people will mostly be willing and glad to do business with him. Note, men who are so filled with confidence, courage, enthusiasm, fearlessness and energy that the moment you come in contact with them you must catch such smart and respond positively. The atmosphere around them is as a result of their constant mental attitude.

This concept has no direct relationship with religion or morality. There are men and women with low level of morality and religious devotion but with positive mental attitude and are able to create such positive environment around them. There are millions of others with profession of high level of religion and morality. Yet they carry negative mental attitude and reflect that all around them.

A man's mental attitude acts as a magnet attracting to him the things, objects, circumstances, environments and people in harmony with that mental attitude. If you think of wealth and prosperity firmly and hold it properly before you, it will build up a constant mental attitude which invariably attracts to you the things conducive to its attainment and materialization. If we hold the ideal of financial success or money, our mental attitude will gradually form and crystallize the money ideal. And the things pertaining to money - people calculated to help us with money, circumstances tending to bring us money, expectation of money.

Fix your mind firmly upon anything, good or bad in the world and you will attract it to you or you are attracted to it in obedience to the universal law of attraction. You attract to you, the things you expect, think about and hold in your mental realm, just as there are air currents in the atmosphere and ocean currents in the seas. Clear your mind of all negative thoughts and fill it with positive, invigorating, helpful, forceful, compelling ideals of success, confidence and expectation of that which you desire. Just as the steel filings fly to the attraction of the magnet, so will that which you need fly to you in response to this great natural principle of mental action - the law of attraction.

MENTAL ACTIVE FORCE

There are two mental attitudes a man may take from. One makes him like a football. It has resilience and reacts strongly when force is applied to it, but it originates nothing; it never acts of itself. There is no power within it. Men of this type are controlled by circumstances and environment; their destinies are decided by things external to themselves. The principle of power within them is never really active at all. They never speak or act from within. This is the attitude of men and women whose lives are lived as reactions to the actions or in actions of other men and their own environment. Man may choose this attitude consciously or unconsciously.

The other attitude makes man like a flowing spring. Power comes out from the center of him. He has within him a well of water springing up into everlasting life, he radiates forces; he is felt by his environment. The principle of power in him is in constant action. He is self-active. This is the attitude of the really intelligent. They can achieve success despite all the odds.

Any man can choose which of the mental attitudes to adopt. Good mental attitude can be cultivated with time and commitment. Good mental attitude can be learnt. Wrong mental attitude can be unlearned.

FAITH AND TRUST

For one to attain financial success he must **first** have faith in himself. **Second**, he must have faith in his fellow men; and **third** faith in the natural principles of financial success.

Without faith in self, one can never accomplish anything and can never influence any other person's opinion of him positively. He cannot also attract to himself the things, persons and circumstances necessary for his welfare. One must learn to believe in himself. People are prone to take a person at his own estimate.

You cannot afford the habit of blind trust- trusting just anybody. Not everybody will be worthy of your trust at the end of the day. Even for the people you have assessed worthy of your trust, that status cannot necessarily be a permanent one. People change. Circumstances change.

However, there cannot be real success in life until you have learnt to trust people. It is your responsibility to select and determine the identity of men and women deserving your trust. Trust also cannot be an excuse to be over optimistic. I have seen people who claim that if you trust people you should not attach importance to documenting business transactions. I have met people who do everything possible to avoid signing agreement in respect of financial transaction. Most time, such people are crafty dubious people. They ask you to **just have faith. Just trust.** Never mind them. That position rests only on either ignorance or deception. Documentation will not solve all the problems, but it will take care of the avoidable ones. The process of documentation and review also affords parties to think through the critical components of the agreement and their likely future implications. It affords parties to properly guide their expectations. One party is able to weigh and align his expectations against the expectations of the other party.

AMBITION

Ambition is the manifestation of mental hunger. It stirs one and makes one feel the inspiration to be up at work doing things, succeeding, creating and accomplishing. It means more than mere eagerness for things. It means deep-seated desire to materialize certain ideals which exist in the mind as mental pictures.

Before one can accomplish anything great, he must possess the relevant ambition. And before he can feel ambition, he must have the preceding hunger which causes him to satisfy it. And so, it follows, anything that will stimulate that mental hunger, will arouse ambition, and thus create that eagerness for action and attainment.

In order for that mental hunger to be manifested, it must have ideals presented to the mind's eye. Just like the gastric juices of the stomach may be stimulated, caused to flow by the sight, smell or thought of food, mental hunger knows nothing better. It is either you have not seen or heard something better or you are mentally lazy. This underscores the connection between positive exposure and ambition.

Ambition is a strong will aroused by a strong desire. The trouble with the majority of the people is that they have been taught that one should take what was given him and be content; but this is not nature's way. Nature implants in each living being a strong desire for that which is necessary for its well-being and nourishment, and a strong will to gratify that natural desire.

By ambition, you are not coveting the things that others have. But you merely desire other things like them. You are willing that these other people should retain their things but are demanding similar good things for yourself.

FIRE OF DESIRE AND WATER OF THE MIND

You can compare desire with the fire that burns brightly beneath the receptacle containing water which later represents the mind. Unless the fire of desire burns brightly and impacts its heat to the water of the mind, there will be nothing but water. But let the fire manifest its ardent energy and heat and then the water converts into steam which turns mighty wheels and drives powerful machinery and in fact "makes things go"

If you can arouse in yourself the fierce, ardent, insatiable desire, you will set in operation one of the nature's most potent mental forces.

Desire is the great moving power of the mind. It is desire that excites into action the will and powers of the individual. It is at the bottom of all effective action, feeling, emotion or expression. "Before a man reaches out to do a thing or to possess a thing, he must first want to and in the degree that the "want to", is felt, so will be his response thereto. Before we love, hate, like or dislike; there must be a desire of some kind. Before we can arouse ambition, there must be a strong desire. Before we can manifest energy, there must be a strong impelling desire."

Do not be sidetracked by any outside factor. It is concentrated desire that produces the greatest power producing steam, which ultimately propels achievements. Keep your mind on that which you want and keep on demanding that which belongs to you, for it is your own.

The universal supply is adequate to meet the needs of everyone, but it responds only to the insistently demanding and the earnestly desiring. Desire creates mental attitude, develops faith, nourishes ambition, unfolds instinctive or latent powers and tends directly and surely towards success. Let the strong dominant desire for financial independence possess you from the tips of your toes to the roots of your hair - feel it ringing through every part of your body and then don't stop until you reach your goals.

MENTAL MAKE OVER THROUGH POSITIVE AFFIRMATION

This is done through the process called Auto-suggestion. Auto-suggestion as used by psychologists means "an impression made upon the mind of another". And here, an "auto - suggestion" is an impression made upon one's own mind in a manner similar to that used in impressing the mind of another. Suggestion is not a matter of argumentative effort but a process of saying a thing so positively, earnestly and convincingly, that the other person takes up the idea, without argument. The principle is the same. One may turn this suggestive die upon the wax of his own mind and by repeated impression may fix certain ideas, qualities and characteristics upon it so that he would have really made himself over to that extent. You know how a man may get to actually believe some old lies that he has been telling for some time. A man may act - out a certain assumed character, until he actually becomes like a creature of new characteristics and qualities that are conducive within himself.

First; you must learn to repeatedly say what you want until your entire system aligns with the formation or creation of it on the inside of you. **Furthermore**, you must also create a mental image of the desired thing. **Then**, you should act out the part you wish to play in a sort of extended preliminary rehearsal by constant thinking of a desired quality of mind, accompanied with the indulgence in the mental picture of yourself as actually possessed of the quality itself. Mental picture accompanied by an "acting out of the part you would like to play" will in due time sow impression and mould your mind to the point that you will actually possess the quality itself.

If you lack ambition for instance, start with constant affirmation like; **"I am ambitious, my ambition grows every day"** and so on. Then, picture yourself in your imagination as being ambitious. See yourself as moving around the world possessed of insatiable ambition which is leading you to strenuous action and wonderful accomplishments. Then, begin to act the part of the ambitious man. Study some ambitious men until you catch their feelings. And then begin to look ambitious, talk in tones of a man possessing ambition, walk like an ambitious man. In short, act out the smallest details.

You don't need to copy the mannerism of the man you have taken for your model. Simply study the man until you can get his feelings, until you can recognize the ambitious emotion and mental attitude animating him and then go to work to feel the same inward feeling. This exercise may be used to acquire any positive qualities you may desire in your life.

For the past twelve years, I have never thought of myself as a poor person. It does not just cross my mind. There are millions of ordinary Nigerians, but I am certainly not one of them. There are poor masses all around, but I am not one of them. This remain settled in my subconscious for over a decade now. It has nothing to do with the amount of physical cash I have per time. Over the years, there have been times I had bills to pay without the slightest idea of where the money would come from. Even that could not change my financial status which was already accepted in my subconscious mind. Over time, nature will work with every other thing around me to bring the position of my pocket or bank account to agree with that status which is already settled in my subconscious.

Over the years, I have also had to study some people with financial freedom mentality until I caught their feelings. At first it was my uncle who was a successful business man. Later it was Elder Felix Ezeh. People generally call him "Lovers". The name "Lovers" is the name of one of his companies. Much later I had to study a CEO of the bank where I worked. Such people don't have to be perfect. Just like you are not perfect. Wisdom enables you to select the character you admire and want to imbibe from any such individuals. You must be very careful not to pick the undesirable character together with the desirable ones. It takes emotional intelligence to be able to remain positive and negative towards an individual, an object or a circumstance at the same time. One other person I have carefully drawn from was Pastor James Ngoka. He was then a Pastor and a

Senior Officer in the Imo State Civil Service. Pastor Ngoka later retired as a Permanent Secretary in Charge of Deputy Governor's Office. I learnt so much about leadership from him in those years. There is a level of wealth and influence you cannot command without strong leadership and emotional intelligence.

I think possibility and act possibility. Even though I have not enjoyed that level of everyday closeness with Reverend Sam Adeyemi, I have taken enough time to study him until I caught his feelings on certain issues of life.

POSITIVE AWARENESS AND HARMONY

For maximum achievement in life, man must be at peace with himself. You must be confident about yourself. You must have personal assurance that God's creation is for you not against you. There are evils in the world. There are goods in the world. What you see is what will come to you. Besides, you cannot solve the problems of the presence of the evils in the world by being excessively conscious of the evil. Many are so conscious of evil that they cannot see the good all around them.

Think about all this until you fully realize all that it means to you. Consider that this is God's world and that it is the best of all possible worlds; that He has brought it thus far toward completion by the processes of organic, social, economic, political and industrial evolution and that it is going on to greater completeness and harmony. Consider that there is only One Source of all things and that source is God.

Think about all this until you see that it is true and until you comprehend how you should live as a citizen of such a wonderful world.

<u>**Next,**</u> convince yourself of the presence of a Universal Intelligence in God's Creation, to which if you align yourself, all things will work together for your good. Think of the wonderful truth that this great intelligence is for you; it is your own intelligence. It is an inner light impelling you toward the right thing and the best thing, the greatest act, and the highest happiness. It is a Principle of Power in you, giving you all the ability and genius there is. It will infallibly guide you to the best if you will submit to it and walk in the light.

Consider what is meant by your consecration of yourself when you say: "I will obey my soul.""I will obey my inner man" This is a sentence of tremendous meaning; it must revolutionize the attitude and behavior of the average person. Think of your identification with this Great Supreme; that all its knowledge is yours, and all its wisdom is yours, for the asking. You are **a god** if you **think like god**. If you think like a god you cannot fail to act like a god. Divine thoughts will surely externalize themselves in a divine life. Thoughts of power will end in a life of power. Great thoughts will manifest in a great personality. Assure yourself that the world and all its resources are for you. They are created to help your development and achievement of worthy goals in life. There is more in the world for you than against you.

Think well of all this, and then you are ready to act.

DRAWING FROM THE INNER MAN

Every person who is ambitious and has a definite objective in life should take a few minutes off each day, and sit alone, giving himself a chance to think, meditate and allow the great rhythmic harmony of nature to flow through his cleared mind and thus gain moments when the outer mind is relaxed and resting, that which is best for us to do.

This process enables you to align the forces of nature to support you in the pursuit of your life's goals. Nature is made to work for you and not against you. The forces of nature, which you are a part of are meant to work for the achievement of your positive goals. This system has been there before you. It is not meant to change for you. Wisdom is for you to align with it.

It is in these quiet moments when the out mind flashes to us that which is best for us to do. We should cultivate this habit in moments of meditation, when we can escape the crowd and thus be able to listen to the voice that sounds from within. By doing this, we place ourselves in harmony with the great universal power from which all original ideas spring into our mental organism ready for use a few moments later when we reemerge into the world of action and of men.

How do you achieve this? Entering into harmony with the universal rhythm of Nature? **First**, your mental attitude must be right. You must have gained control over your thoughts and words so that your mind is open and receptive to the great good of the world. Your mind must be free of hatred and all form of discouragement. Avoid all pessimism, negative thoughts, cringing, worms of the dust mentality or poverty thought. Your frame of mind must be that of good-will, encouragement, optimism with positive thoughts expectant of wealth, prosperity and all good things that man hear of the universe and is entitled to by right of his sonship. Remember **we are all His offspring**. He is for us and not against us. God is for you and not against you. His world is made for you and you are a rightful citizen of the universe.

He loves us, He does not hate us. This mental attitude will surround you with a personal thought atmosphere which repels from you the negative or evil things and attracts to you the positive or good things of life. This positive thought atmosphere is what the author has earlier referred to as **positive internal environment**.

When you are satisfied that your personal atmosphere is right, then each day, preferably between twelve and one o'clock, or if that time is not convenient, anytime early in the morning, close the doors of your room for a few moments. Ensure you would not be disturbed. Then free your mind from the fear of interruption and disturbance. Take a position of restful and peaceful calm. Relax every muscle and take the tension off every nerve. Take a few deep restful breathes which will seem like great sights and will tend to relax your body and mind. Then detach your thoughts inward upon yourself. Shut out all the material cares, worries and problems of the day and sink into a mental state of peaceful calm.

Think "I open myself to the inflow of the universal rhythmic harmony." You will soon begin to feel a sense of relationship with that harmony coming into you. Filling your mind and body with feelings of rest and peace and latent power; you will soon come to a sense of new strength and energy and a desire to once more emerge upon the sense of duties. Assure yourself that the resources of the universe are made for you, to assist you in the pursuit of your positive desires. The world is for you not against you. You must also assure yourself that you were created for the greater good of the universe. Hence, all resources for that purpose are already made available for you. They are in the world. They are accessible to you and reachable by you.

Then close the meditation on this point. Then go forth with your new energy, filled with the vibrations of the universe. And you will see how refreshed and vigorous you are and how your mind leaps eagerly and enthusiastically to the task before it. Then follow with words of affirmation drawn from scriptures and those from other men of great achievement whom you have chosen to admire.

This practice is essential to financial success and success in other realms of life. A few moments spent with your inner self and the great universal power each day, if practiced assiduously will establish within you the creative mind. It is advised that you have writing materials to take note of ideas that will run across your mind at such moment. Learn to always go back to them for further processing.

"This marks the difference between the peasant who pledge along from day to day without a new idea for his own or humanity's betterment and the man at the top who "does things". The constructive man who builds rail, roads, steamship, large mercantile establishment and who furnishes funds to carry the great work of the world along; both of these men are needed, but it feels better to be near the top." The more you practice the more you will open up that great subconscious reservoir of yours which is overflowing with original ideas. Over time, you will gain the power to get in touch with your inner self and tap its reservoir. You may be in the street, car, out for a walk, while you are sharing and there will flash through to your conscious minds in vivid outlines, ideas that when worked out will mean your money and financial independence. Write such ideas down for further processing.

MENTAL CREATION

One of the greatest secrets of great and successful people in the world is their awareness that everything in the world is created twice. According to Reverend Sam Adeyemi, the first creation is in the mind. This is followed by manifestation in the physical structures and activities that are accessible by our physical eyes.

"Think of the mighty bridges spanning the rivers across our modern cities. Consider each strand of steel, each support, each bit of construction and the whole bridge in its entirety." Great buildings which rear their imposing forms and shapes along our business streets were created in the minds of their architects and actually existed in their minds before the buildings could be erected physically.

With reference to my earlier examples, VGC was first built in somebody or some people's mind before it turned to physical city. Eko Atlantic City, Aso Rock Villa or even the City of Abuja all existed in human minds before taking physical forms. Most of the beautiful cities and structure around the world were built first in the human minds. Think of all big and small business enterprises and companies. Think of wonderful worship centers all over Nigeria. They all existed first as mental pictures. All government systems and institutions are all products of human minds.

Above statements are more or less common place, but the

majority of people overlook them and down play their importance. They ignore the fact that anything and everything that has ever been created in the material form must of necessity have been created in mental form previously in the mind of the person creating it. Everything that you can see or think of that has been made, has first been created mentally, in its every part and as a whole.

This is true of financial success just as it is true of everything else. Some build little by little, seeing only just a little in advance of their building and thus do their mental creation by piece-meal. Others see the whole thing in general outlines and then fill in the details in both cases. To achieve financial success, you must learn to form a mental picture of what you want and then apply every effort to fill in the picture. "You must have a picture of money, see yourself using it, handling it, spending it, acquiring more and thus going through all the motions of the man of money, you must paint a great mental picture of wealth and then start to work to fill in the picture and to bring it to physical reality." Your perception of money must be right. It must not be seen as anything mysterious. It is a tool for your use. It is available in the world in enough quantity for all the inhabitants of the world. The gap between you and the money you need are time and specific intelligent actions.

The problem with the majority of poor people is that they fail to engage the power of their imagination. Their dreams, if they have dream at all, are based on available money or other resources. The rich man is the one that settles what he wants first, at the level of imagination. At that level, there is no limitation. It makes it possible for you to consciously acquire the required strong desire, passion and faith to bring your dream to physical reality. When your imagination is engaged within your cultivated environment of positive mental attitude, you find working in you the power of great possibility. The great successful men of the world have used their imaginations, instead of despising them. They think ahead and create their mental picture, and then go to work bringing the picture to physical reality in all its details. Their efforts are then geared towards filling in here, adding a little there, altering this a bit and that a bit steadily building.

If you would attain sustainable wealth, you must become a **mental creator** and designer of that which you long for as well as a **material builder.** The two must go hand in hand and work for financial abundance.

No one is condemned to the lower levels of life by circumstances or lack of opportunity. The principle of power in man is sufficient for all the requirements of his soul. No possible combination of circumstances can keep him down if he makes his personal attitude right and determine to rise.

The power which formed man and purposed him for growth also controls the circumstances of society, industry and government. And this power is never divided against itself. The power which is in you is in the things around you, and when you begin to move forward, the things around you will arrange themselves for your advantage.

Man was formed for growth, and all things external were designed to promote his growth. No sooner does a man awakens his soul and enter on the advancing way than he finds that not only is God for him, but nature, society and his fellow men are for him also; and all **things work together for his good** if he obeys the natural law.

BIGGER PICTURE

"Poverty is no bar to greatness, for poverty can always be removed. Martin Luther, as a child sang in the street for bread. Linnaeus the naturalist, had only forty dollars with which to educate himself; he mended his own shoes and often has to beg meals from his friends. Hugh Miller apprenticed to a stone mason, began to study geology in a quarry. George Stephenson, inventor of locomotive engine, and one of the greatest of civil engineers, was a local miner, working in mine, when awakened and began to think. James watt was a sickly child and was not strong enough to be sent to school. Abraham Lincoln was a poor boy". Young Obafemi Awolowo had to beg Chief Timothy Odutola for a loan to pursue his Law course in Britain, a request which was turned down. Dr. Nnamdi Azikwe was said to have attempted suicide as a boy, because of frustration. In each of these cases we see a principle of power in the man which lifts him above all opposition and adversity.

There is a principle of power in you. If you use it and apply it in a certain way you can overcome all heredity, to become a great and powerful personality. When you find yourself in a negative external environment, your duty to yourself is to cultivate a positive internal environment. If you are consistent, your internal environment will soon prevail over your external environment and circumstances. **"As a man thinks in his heart, so is he."**

POWER OF IMAGINATION

I have chosen the story below from Napoleon Hell's Book " Think and Grow Rich"

"Some thirty years ago a young clergy man by the name of Gunsaulus announced in the newspapers of Chicago that he would preach a sermon the following Sunday Morning entitled:

"WHAT I WOULD DO IF I HAD A MILLION DOLLAR!"

The announcement caught the eye of Phillip D. Armour, the wealthy packing- house king, who decided to hear the sermon.

In the sermon Dr. Gunsaulus pictured a great school of technology where young men and young women could be taught how to succeed in life by developing the ability to THINK in practical rather than in theoretical terms; where they would be taught to "learn by doing". "If I had a million dollars," "said the young preacher, " I would start such a school."

After the sermon was over Mr. Armour walked down the aisle to the pulpit, introduced himself, and said, "Young man, I believe you could do all you said you could, and if you will come down to my office tomorrow morning I will give you the million dollars you need.

There is always plenty of capital for those who can create practical plans for using it. That was the beginning of the Armour Institute of Technology, one of the very practical schools of the country. The school was born in the "imagination" of a young man who never would have been heard of outside of the community in which he preached had it not been for the "imagination," plus the capital of Phillip D. Armour. The capital had always been there but it was the power of imagination that brought it to Gunsaulus. If he had failed to use his imagination, the money would still be there but will never be available to Gunsaulus. It would probably have been attracted to other persons with positive imagination or it would have remained with Phillip D. Armour

Every great railroad, and every outstanding financial institution and every mammoth business enterprise, and every great invention, began in the imagination of some person.

F.W Woolworth created the Five and Ten Cent Store Plan in his "imagination" before it became a reality and made him a multimillionaire.

Thoma A. Edison created the talking machine and the moving picture and the incandescent electric light bulb and scores of other useful inventions, in his own "imagination," before they became a reality.

"During the Chicago fire, scores of merchants whose stores went up in the smoke stood near the smoldering embers of their former places of business, grieving over their loss. Many of them decided to go away into other cities and start over again. In the group was Marshall Field, who saw in his own "imagination," the world's greatest retail store, standing on the selfsame spot where his former store had stood, which was then but a ruined mass of smoking timbers. That store became a reality.

Fortunate is the young man or young woman who learns, early in life, to use imagination, and doubly so in this age of greater opportunity.

Wherever you are, whoever you are, whatever you may be following as an occupation, there is room for you to make yourself more useful, and in that manner more productive, by developing and using your "imagination".

Thousands of people walked over the great Calumet Copper Mine without discovering it. Just one lone man used his "imagination", dug down into the earth a few feet, investigated, and discovered the richest copper deposit on earth.

You and every other person walk, at one time or another, over your "Calumet Mine". Discovery is a matter of investigation and use of "imagination". This book may lead the way to your "Calumet," and you may be surprised when you discover that you were standing right over this rich mine, in the work in which you are now engaged.

In his lecture on "Acres of Diamonds," Russell Conwell tells us that we need not seek opportunity in the distance that we may find it right where we stand! THIS IS A TRUTH WELL WORTH REMEMBERING!" Napoleon Hill, 1928

PERSONAL EXPERIENCE ON MENTAL CREATION

Not long after I relocated to Lagos in January 2009, I made up my mind that I was going to live in one of the prime areas of Lagos Island. The city of Lagos is broadly segmented into two - Lagos Island and Lagos Mainland. Lagos Island is generally believed to be expensive and to have more concentration of the middle class and the rich class. Of course, there are a number of elite expensive areas also in Lagos Mainland. But it is generally believed that Lagos Island has more concentration of the rich and middle class. I started out in Ikorodu, one of the suburbs on Lagos Mainland.

As soon as I set Lagos Island as my destination, the picture of the area and the type of life I wanted to live was clear in my mind. It took me some years but today it is a reality.

The acquisition of our property in Lekki clearly demonstrates the unfailing power of imagination and mental creation. I started out at the time it was difficult for me to pay the rent for the duplex we occupied in Oregun, Lagos Mainland.

A change in Group Management in my office came with many obnoxious and unfavorable policies which lead to the suspension of some of our annual allowances. At the same time, I was forced to pay down a loan which I obtained in the office to acquire a small investment apartment in Abuja. It became very difficult for me that year to raise N1 million for my rent.

At the same time I had a clear picture of the type of house I desired to own as a residence. This unfortunate situation had come at the time I had clearly formed a clear picture of what I wanted. The full picture had taken me some years to fully form. I also had a clear picture of the type of area I wanted to live. It then appeared to me as if I was too ambitious in the choice I had earlier made in my mind. I was tempted to start developing a plot of land I had earlier acquired in Ikorodu. I engaged architects and engineers to produce drawings of what I had in my mind, hoping to at least start constructing my dream home on my land in Ikorodu. I engaged architects to draw and redraw my idea. The drawing was done three different times by different architects, yet I felt none of them was able to capture the picture I had in my mind.

In the midst of these, the picture of the place and property remains clear in my mind. Then I decided to continue with the pursuit of my heart desire despite the financial difficulties of that time. To reinforce my belief along this line, I decided to go on the survey of the area in which I have decided to acquire the property. I drove to Lekki on Sunday afternoons after church service. Later I started driving there along with my wife and children, telling them how we would soon move to Lekki as residents. That was a time I could not boast of N1million in physical cash. Not long after this, we moved into the stage of pricing properties in the area. I priced many properties that have some resemblance of the one in my imagination. I also made different offers. Some were accepted while others were rejected. My wife, property owners and agents never knew that I did not have the money saved somewhere. They all took my proposals very seriously. I also was serious about buying a house. Only that the physical money was not available.

The day we went to check the house where we now live, it was almost a match of the picture I had in my mind which my Architects and Engineers were not able to capture all along.

"You are a thinking center in original substance, and the thoughts of original substance have creative power; whatever is formed in its thought and held as a thought –

form, must come into existence as a visible and so - called material form, and a thought-form held in thinking substance is a reality; it is a real thing, whether it has yet become visible to mortal eye or not.

This is a fact that you should impress upon your understanding that a thought held in thinking substance is a real thing; a form, and has actual existence, although it is not visible to you. You internally take the form in which you think of yourself; and you surround yourself with the invisible forms of those things with which you associate in your thoughts.

If you desire a thing, picture it clearly and hold the picture steadily in mind until it becomes a definite thought-form; and if your practices are not such as to separate you from God, the thing you want will come to you in material form. It must do so in obedience to the law by which the universe was created." Wallace D. Wattles 1907

Of Course that was not the first time I have had a picture in my heart coming to be produced in the physical. There are many of such experiences I have got over the years.

My study of the works of individuals of great mind like Napoleon Hill, Wallace D. Wattles and McGraw Hill merely reinforced my belief in the power of imagination and mental creation.

Your duty is to study this book with appropriate concentration. Study it over and over again until the messages become your own. I can guarantee your financial life will be transformed. The transformation is guaranteed by the operation of universal law.

THOUGHTS ARE THINGS

GREATNESS is only attained by the constant thinking of great thoughts. No man can become great in outward personality until he is great internally; and no man can be great internally until he THINKS. No amount of education, reading, or study can make you great without thought; but thought can make you great with very little study or formal education. Thought is the chief molder of your internal environment. Your internal environment controls everything about you at the long run.

There are altogether too many people who are trying to make something of themselves, by reading books without thinking; all such will fail. You are not mentally developed by what you read, but by what you think about what you read. The greatest good this book will do in you is to stir up your critical thinking process.

Thinking is the hardest and most exhausting of all labor; and hence many people shrink from it. God has so formed us that we continuously impelled to thought; we must either think or engage in some activity to escape thought. The headlong, continuous chase for pleasure in which most people spend all their leisure time is mostly an effort to escape thought. If they are alone, or if they have nothing amusing to take their attention, as a novel to read or a show to see, they must think; And to escape from thinking they resort to novels, shows and all the endless devices of the purveyors of amusement. This is one area where the television, home videos and today's entertainment industry do more harm than good. Most people spend the greater part of their leisure time running away from thought, hence they are where they are. We never move forward until we begin to think.

Read less and think more. Read about great things and think about great questions and issues. We have at the present time few really great figures in the political life of our country; our politicians are a petty lot. The way the 2015 election campaigns went is a pointer to the fact that not many Nigerian electorates and political office seekers are good thinkers. The elections were long gone before Nigerians started asking questions. Many of the electorates are gullible. We had more noise all over the places than issue based engagement. Today, even Professors of English Language in Nigeria are tempted to check dictionary for the meaning of the word "CHANGE". There are no Lincoln, no Webster, no Clay, Calhoun, or Jackson. There are no many Obafemi Awolowos today.

Why? Because our present statesmen deal only with sordid and petty issues. - Questions of naira and Kobo, of expediency and party success, of material prosperity without regards to ethical right. Thinking along these lines does not call forth great souls. The statesmen of Lincoln's time and previous times dealt with questions of eternal truth, of human rights and justice. These men thought upon great themes; they thought great thoughts, and they became great men.

Thinking, not mere knowledge or information, makes personality. Thinking is growth; you cannot think without growing. You cannot truely grow without thinking.

Every thought engenders another thought. Write one idea and others will follow until you have written a page. You cannot fathom your own mind; it has neither bottom nor boundaries. Your first thoughts may be crude; but as you go on thinking you will discover more and more of yourself; you will develop new faculties. Heredity, environment, circumstances and, all such things must give way before you if you practice sustained and continuous thought. Your thinking forms your internal environment and your internal environment rules everything about you. On the other hand, if you neglect to think for yourself and only use other people's thoughts, you will never know what you are capable of; and you will end by being incapable of anything.

There can be no real greatness without original thought. All that a man does outwardly is the expression and completion of his inward thinking. No great action is possible until a great thought has preceded it. Action is the second form of thought, and personality is the materialization of thought. Environment is the result of thought; things group themselves and arrange themselves around you according to your thought. "There is, as Emerson says, some central idea or conception of yourself by which all the facts of your life are arranged and classified. Change this central idea and you change the arrangement or classification of all the facts and circumstances of your life.

"You are paid to think. You are not paid to do". said Dr. Victor Oladokun at the CEO Class 2017, organized by Success Power Media International, Lagos.

You are what you are because of what you think. You will eventually become like what you continue to thing about.

GREATNESS BY THOUGHT

You will never become great until your own thoughts make you great, therefore it is of the first importance that you should THINK.

You will never do great things in the external world until you think great things in your internal world. There must also be a great goal or objective to which you are committed. To think great thoughts you must be absolutely sincere; and to be sincere you must know that your intentions are right. Insincere or false thinking is never great, however logical and brilliant it may be. The undoing of many people of our generation is that they never have original thoughts. Some are only very afraid of original thoughts. This mindset stems from the fact that majority are not ready to take personal responsibility. Therefore, they would rather go by what have been thought out by other people.

The **first** and most important step is to seek the truth about human relations, to know what you ought to be to other men, and what they ought to be to you. You should study organic and social evolution. THINK; think the whole matter over until you see the world of things and men in the right way. THINK about what God has done until you can SEE what HE is doing.

Your **next** step is to think yourself into the right personal attitude. Your viewpoint tells you what the right attitude is, and obedience to the soul puts you into it. It is only by making a complete consecration of yourself to the highest that is within you that you can attain to sincere thinking. So long as you know you are selfish in your aims, or dishonest or crooked in any way in your intentions or practices, your thinking will be false and your thoughts will have no power. THINK about the way you are doing things; about all your intentions, purposes and practices until you know that they are right.

"Whatsoever things are true, whatsoever things are honest, whatsoever things are just, whatsoever things are pure, whatsoever things are lovely, whatsoever things are of good report; if there be any virtue, and if there be any

praise, think on these things" Philippians 4:8 KJV

You must get to a point where you have eliminated all forms of doubts and fear about propriety of the purpose of your major assignment per time. Be sure what you are doing per time is fulfillment or at least part fulfillment of your life assignment. Be sure what you are committed to is of ultimate benefit to humanity and God. Have this at the back of your mind; God and His creations are there to assist you in the achievement of your noble objective. The world is for you and not against you.

Are there enemies in the world?

Yes. The ultimate truth however is that, what is for you is more, more potent and more powerful than what is against you. Your duty is to give attention to what is for you and not what is against you. **"Greater is he that is in you than he that is in the world."** 1 John 4:4. Every man is defined by what is in him, not what is in the world. What is in you sets the limits. Better still, you set the limit based on what is in you. Where there is doubt, get rid of it. Where there is fear, get rid of it. By this practice, you move all the divine resources in the world to your favour.

The fact of his own complete unity with God is one that no person can grasp without deep and sustained thinking. Anyone can accept the proposition in a superficial way, but to feel and realize a vital comprehension of it is another matter. It is easy to think of going outside of yourself to meet God, but it is not so easy to think of going inside yourself to meet God. But God is there, and in the holy of holies of your own soul you may meet Him face to face. It is a tremendous thing; this fact that all you need is already within you; that you do not have to consider how to get the power to do what you want to do or to make yourself what you want to be. You have only to consider how to use the power you have in the right way.

The function of the will is to direct thought. Think about the good side of men; the lovely, attractive part and exert your will in refusing to think of anything else in connection with them. It is a great thing to love men so and this is only achieved by thought. Nothing can make you great but thought.

"All truly wise thoughts have been thought already thousands of times; but to make them really ours we must think them over again honestly till they take root in our personal expression."
- Goethe.

"All that a man is outwardly is but the expression and completion of his inward thought. To work effectively he must think clearly; to act nobly."
- Channing.

"Great men are they who see that spirituality is stronger than any material force; that thoughts rule the world."
- Emerson

"Some people study all their lives, and at their death they have learned everything except to think."
- Domergue.

"It is the habitual thought that frames itself into our life. It affects us even more than our intimate social relations do. Our confidential friends have not so much to do in shaping our lives as the thoughts have which we harbor?"
- J. W. Teal.

"When God lets loose a great thinker on this planet, then all things are at risk. There is not a piece of science but its flank may be turned tomorrow; nor any literary reputation or the so-called eternal names of fame that may not be refused and condemned."
- Emerson

Chapter Nine

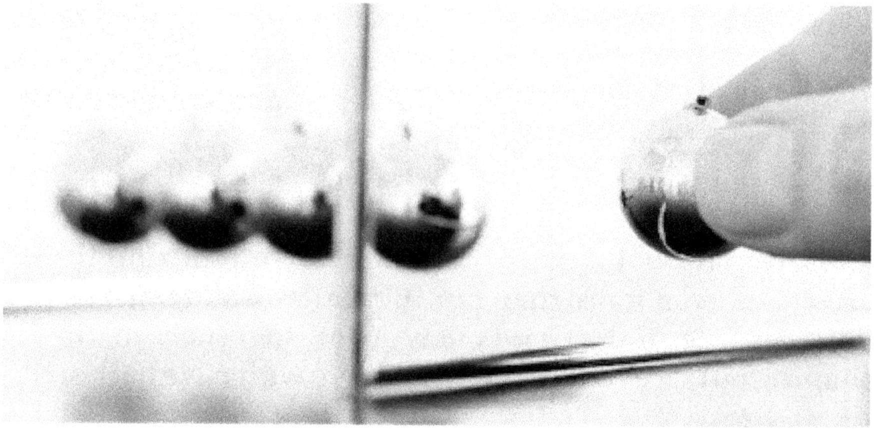

Wealth Impact

Contents of this chapter are direct continuations of the last chapter. We continue here by dealing with issues of life which people generally view in isolation but with direct impacts on outcomes of people's financial life. When subject of money is mentioned, majority of people think about job, employment, trade, investment, business, profession and so on. Not many people realize that your emotional intelligence is as important to money making as the job or business you engage in. Two persons are in the same trade. One is rich while the other is poor. They may even be in the same business location and environment. Two people can even work for the same organization, at the same level and the same remuneration. One becomes financially successful while the other has the opposite outcome. Henry Ford worked with others in Edison's workshop. How come we only heard about Ford many years later? Many things might have been responsible for difference in the outcomes. However, the most likely factors are those that are embedded in emotion attitude and the value system of affected individuals.

We therefore continue to deal with some of these emotional issues and how they relate to money making and wealth building.

POWER OF CONCENTRATION

English dictionary defines "concentration as the act or process of bringing or directing things towards a common center and thereby condensing and intensifying the force of the things". The key things to note is that there is great power in "bringing forces to a common center"

We can never expect to win in anything unless we firmly concentrate our minds upon the things we seek. You need to make your mental picture of what you want, and then start to desire it as hard as you are able to. By so doing you will concentrate your attention, energy and will upon that thing until something happens. You must learn to concentrate your powers and will upon the things you want and then to keep the steady focus day by day, never allowing yourself to be side tracked or swerved from your main object of desire, interest and will.

This is the key to financial success and attainment of success in other areas of life. Your goal must be clear enough that you direct all your energy at it per time. Never expect sustainable financial success without a clear objective to attain such financial success. We talk here of 'objective' and not a 'wish'. There is this belief in my native place that 'wealth is blind'. Nothing can be farther from the truth. Love may be blind but true wealth is never blind. Rather, it is the people who think wealth is blind that are actually blind. They are blind because they cannot recognize the clear ways that wealth follow.

It is not unlikely to have more than one thing requiring attention at the same time. The truth is that they cannot all have equal importance. Your first personal duty is to allocate available resources, particularly time and energy, based on your established values and priority. You then owe yourself the duty of determination and strong will to keep to your allocated resources without allowing distractions. The greatest undoing of most poor men in our generation is their failure to set the right values and priority. This is particularly when it comes to socialization and recreation. If you have the objective of financial abundance, you cannot afford to attend every social function. You cannot attend even all those that are important. There are many recreational activities people engage in without actually recreating. You must identify such in your own case and avoid them. This will enable you to save your time and energy and concentrate them on those things that are fundamental to the attainment of your financial goals.

One should begin by practicing concentration on little things, until he masters them and then he may move on to the consideration and contemplation of larger things. It is quite an art to be able to do one thing at a time, to the exclusion of distracting thoughts and objects. The best workmen along any line of human efforts are those who are able to concentrate on their work and practically lose themselves in their tasks **for the time being**. There are phone calls you must learn to avoid while you are actively working at your set goal. For most wealthy people of our time, even the usual complementary and reassurance calls from their spouses cannot be at anytime of the day. You must get to a point where only calls that are directly related to the task at hand and those that cannot be deferred are receive or attend to.

The first step in gaining concentration begins with the control of attention. Master the attention and you have acquired the art of concentration. By holding your attention upon a thing, you direct to it all your mental forces.

You can concentrate on anything you are intensely interested in, or dearly love. Your next duty will be to allocate specific time to such a thing and keep such time with discipline.

PERSISTENCE

There is need for a steady, determined, persistent application of concentration to the one object upon which you have set your mind. Having found the object of your desire and knowing how to concentrate upon it, you should then learn how to be persistent in your concentration, aim and purpose. There is nothing like sticking to a thing. Many men are brilliant, resourceful and industrious but they fail to reach the goal by reason of their lack of **"stick-to-it-iveness"**. You should acquire the tenacity of the bulldog, and refuse to be shaken off of a thing once you have fixed your attention and desire upon it. This is my ninth year of work on this book. I have put so much work and thoughts into the project which gives me the confidence that every diligent reader will have his life shaped for financial success by reading this book, with required concentration and persistent practice of the principles taught in it. The title has had to change a few times over the years, but the subject has remained the same.

One must learn to acquire that consistent, unvarying, unrelenting `application to the object of his desire that will enable him to hold his will firmly on the object until it is shaped according to his wishes.

Buxton said **"The longer I live, the more certain I am that**

the great difference between men, between the feeble and the powerful, the great and the insignificant is Energy - invisible determination - a purpose once fixed and then death or victory." That quality will do anything that can be done in this world. It will rule over talents and natural gifts. It will conquer undue advantages and privileges.

"Resolve is what makes a man manifest; not puny resolve, not crude determination; not errant purpose - but that strong and indefatigable will which treads down difficulties and danger, as a boy threads down the hearing first lands of winter, which kindles his eyes and brain with a proud pulse - beat towards the unattainable. Will makes men giants"
- Donald G. Mitchell.

"I have brought myself by long meditation to the conviction that a human being with a settled purpose must accomplish it, and that nothing can resist a will which will stake even existence upon its fulfillment".
- Disreali

"When a firm decisive spirit is recognized, it is curious to see how the space clears around a man and leaves him room and freedom."
- John Foster.

"Courage to me is doing something daring, no matter how afraid, insecure, intimidated, alone, unworthy, incapable, ridiculed or whatever paralyzing emotion you might feel.

Courage is taking action...... no matter what. So you're afraid? Be afraid. Be scared silly to the point you're trembling and nauseous, but do it anyway."
- Richelle E. Goodrich.

If you lack persistence, you should begin to train yourself in the direction of acquiring the habit of sticking to things. This practice will establish a new habit of the mind, and will also tend to cause the appropriate brain cells to develop and thus give to you a permanent characteristics of the desired quality, that you are seeking to develop.

HABIT

"It has been said that all men are "the creatures of habit" and that habit is a cable, we weave a thread of it each day, and it becomes so strong that we cannot break it". This statement comes out of the notion that habit becomes a cruel tyrant ruling and compelling men against their will, desire and inclination. The truth is that this reflects only one part of the potentials of human habit. The power of habit can also be harnessed and controlled in the service of man, just as have other forces of nature. It is possible for man to master habit and set it to work instead of being a slave to it.

According to modern psychologists, habit may be certainly, harnessed and set to work, instead of being allowed to dominate one's action and characters. Just as bad habits are usually formed unconsciously, good habits can be formed consciously and with the intention of aiding the achievement of positive personal objects.

Thousands of people have applied this knowledge and have turned the force of habit into new channels, and have compelled it to work their machinery of action, instead of being allowed to run to waste, or else permitted to sweep away the structures that men have erected with care and expense or destroy fertile mental fields.

A habit is a **"mental path"** over which our actions have traveled for some time each passing making the path a little deeper and a little wider. If you have to walk over a field or through a forest, you know how natural it is for you, to choose the clearest path in preference to the less worn ones. And greatly in preference to stepping out across the field through the woods and making a new path. The line of mental action is just the same. **It is movement along the lines of the least resistance- passage over the well - worn path.**

Habits are created by repetition and formed in accordance to a natural law, observable in all animate things as well. Rivers and streams of water cut their paths through the land and thereafter flow along the habit path. The law is in operation everywhere. The best way in which old habits may be removed is to form new habits to counteract and replace the old undesirable ones. Form new mental paths over which to travel and the old ones will soon become less distinct and in time will practically fill up from disuse. Each time you travel over the path of the desirable mental habit, you make the path deeper and wider and make it so much easier to travel it thereafter. At the same time, you are making the old path less distinct or less easy to follow.

This mental path is a very important thing and I cannot overemphasize the need to start making the desirable mental paths over which you wish to travel Practice, practice and practice being a good path maker.

Any habit may be discontinued by building in its place some other and more desirable habits. Wrong "spending" habit must be replaced by the "saving" habit by all who attain financial independence.

Mere discontinuation of an undesirable habit is not enough as such habits have a tendency to reappear unless the place they formerly occupied in the mind is filled by some other habits of a different nature.

The discontinuance of a habit leave a "hole" in the mind, and this hole must be filled up with some other forms of habit or the old one will return and claim its place. Poor planning or lack of planning must be replaced with habit of planning and commitment to execution of plans.

SELFWORTH

I believe that there is nothing too good for the man and woman who assert their right to live and partake of the good thing of this world. For anyone to achieve abundance, he must first believe that abundance is the right that nature has offered to him as a **'free citizen'** of the world. This status is freely bestowed on you by the Creator. You don't have to qualify for it. Your only duty is to believe and walk in the consciousness of your status. That sense of right does need to come from the belief that the world is created for you just as it is created for other dwellers of the earth. And that you have fundamental right to partake of the good resources of the earth.

"There was a French soldier who carried a dispatch to Emperor Napoleon and whose horse dropped dead from fatigue as he sprang from it and handed the Emperor the dispatch which he had carried from miles away. Napoleon wrote an answer, and dismounting from his own horse handed the bridle to the soldier saying "take this horse, ride back, comrade." "Nay," cried the soldier as he gazed at the blooded horse and his trappings. "It is too magnificent and grand for me, a common soldier." "Take it" cried Napoleon, "there is nothing too grand and magnificient for a soldier of France".

And these words, rapidly repeated through the ranks and columns of his army, gave to his tired troops a new and fresh inspiration and energy."Nothing too grand and magnificent for a soldier of France", they said, and the thought that "they were such worthy individuals inspired them to the almost miraculous deeds that followed. Napoleon understood human nature, and the laws of psychology.

Tell a man that he is a worm of the dust and deserving of nothing but kicks and punishment, and if he believes you he will sink to the mental level of the worm and will cringe and crawl and eat dirt. But let him know that he has within him the divine spark and that there is nothing too good for him, nothing that he has not a right to aspire to, no heights which are not his own if he but climb to them. Tell him these things, I say and he will become a transfigured creature, ready and willing to attempt great things and do mighty deeds. "**As a man thinketh in his heart so is he" Proverbs 23:7 KJV**

Assure yourself that you have a right to all the good things of this world. You are a worthy human being and not a crawling thing of the dust. Raise up your head and look the world in the eyes, affirming your relationship with the **Divine Cause** that brought you into being and asserting your right to partake of your heritage from that **Power**. Nature comes to the aid and assistance of the strong individuals who assert their right to live and prosper. Nature tries in every way to build up strong, confident, self-reliant, self – respecting individuals. It reserves the prizes of life for the strong hands that have courage to reach out and take their place, instead of those cringing, shrinking personalities that cower and shiver back in the corner, afraid to call their souls their own.

Align your mind to the truth that the good things of the earth have been placed here for man's use and for his development and happiness. There is nothing too good for men and women, for they are the rightful inheritors and heirs of their Creator.

The Power that called us into being has placed in this world of ours all that is necessary for our well-being and has implanted in our hearts the natural hunger for nourishment, physical, mental and spiritual. This very hunger is Nature's promise that there exists that which is intended to satisfy it. That which you need and for which you are hungry, exists for you. It is yours and you are not robbing others when you seek for it and draw it to you. There is enough in our universe to satisfy all legitimate desires of man.

HEIRS OF GOD'S CREATION

The posture of bold assertion of your right to this world's goods is contrary to many of our modern day teaching on humility. It contradicts the isolated belief that **"we are pilgrims and strangers in this world"**. The fact of our being pilgrims and strangers in this world is only applicable in the sense that God is the Creator and the Ultimate Owner of the world goods rather than men.

The balanced truth of the scripture is that the **"creation (nature/universe) waits earnestly for the manifestation of**

the sons of God" Romans 8:19. I believe a key aspect of that manifestation is our confident assertion of our status as heirs to the creation of God. Of course, the "sons of God" in the Bible in a sense refers to those who have received sonship through faith in Christ. But the scripture acknowledges in another sense that we are all "**His offspring" Acts 17:28, 29**. If you can embrace the truth that all creation including man originated from the same source and the truth that man was created in the image of God, it becomes easier for you to work in consciousness of your right to the good things of the world. Man was created to take charge of God's creation. Embedded in nature is all that man requires for his status.

"He has given unto us all things pertaining to life and godliness." Everything you need for full expression of your potential is already available in the world. And by nature those resources are attracted to you. By nature also, you are attracted to those resources. What this revelation will do is to help you position yourself in such a way that your disposition, expectation habits and actions will facilitate these naturally orchestrated attractions rather than obstruct them.

GRATITUDE

Many people who order their lives rightly in all other ways are kept in poverty by their lack of gratitude. Having received one gift from God, they cut the wires which connect them with Him by failing to make acknowledgement. It is easy to understand that the nearer we live to the source of wealth, the more we shall receive. It is easy also to understand that the soul that is always grateful lives in closer touch with God than the one which never looks to Him in thankful acknowledgement. The more gratefully we fix our minds on the **'Supreme'** when good things come to us, the more good things we will receive, and the more rapidly they will come. The reason simply is that the mental attitude of gratitude draws the mind into closer touch with the Source from which the blessings come.

If it is a new thought to you that gratitude brings your whole mind into closer harmony with the Creative Energies of the universe, consider it well, and you will see that it is true. The good things you already have come to you along the line of obedience to certain laws. Gratitude will lead your mind out along the ways by which things come; and it will keep you in close harmony with **creative thoughts** and prevent you from falling into **competitive thoughts**. Competitive thought is where you run on a consciousness that your success and that of another person are mutually exclusive. You can have what you desire without denying the other person that already has the same the use of his own. There is enough in the world to go round.

Gratitude alone can keep you looking towards the ALL, and

prevents you from falling into the error of thinking of the supply is limited or scarce. And to do that would be fatal to your hope.

There is the Law of Gratitude, and it is absolutely necessary that you should observe the law, if you are to get the results you seek. The law of gratitude is the natural principle that actions and reactions are always equal, and in opposite directions. The grateful outreaching of your mind in thankful praise to the God is a liberation or expenditure of force; it cannot fail to reach that to which it is addressed, and the reaction is an instantaneous movement towards you.

"Draw nigh unto God, and He will draw nigh unto you." That is a statement of spiritual and psychological truth.

And if your gratitude is strong and constant, the reaction is the movement of the things you want always toward you. Notice the grateful attitude that Jesus took; how He always seems to be saying, **"I thank Thee, Father, that Thou heareth me".** Many negative tendencies like unforgiveness, greed, pride and stinginess are all traceable to lack of grateful hearts. And these are forces that drive man farther from his Source - God.

You cannot exercise much power without gratitude; for it is gratitude that keeps you connected with power.
But the value of gratitude does not consist solely in getting

you more blessings in the future. Without gratitude you cannot keep from dissatisfied thought for long regarding things as they are. "The moment you permit your mind to dwell with dissatisfaction upon things as they are, you begin to lose ground. You fix attention upon the common, the ordinary, the poor, and the squalid and mean; and your mind takes the form of these things. Then you will transmit these forms or mental images to the creative power within you and the common, the poor, the squalid, and mean will come to you."

To permit your mind to dwell upon the inferior is to become inferior and to surround yourself with inferior things. On the other hand, to fix your attention on the best is to surround yourself with the best, and to become the best. The creative Power within us makes us into the image of that to which we give our attention. We are Thinking Substance and thinking substance always takes the form of that which it thinks about. If you fix your attention on poverty and lack, this is what you will attract. If you fixed your attention on wealth, it will certainly come to you in a matter of time. The grateful mind is constantly fix upon the best; therefore it tends to become the best; it takes the form or character of the best; and will receive the best.

Also, faith is born of gratitude. The grateful mind continually expects good things, and expectation becomes faith. The reaction of gratitude upon one's own mind produces faith; and every outgoing wave of grateful thanksgiving increases faith. He who has no feeling of gratitude cannot long retain a living faith; and without a living faith you cannot get rich by the creative method. It is necessary, then to cultivate the habit of being grateful for every good thing that comes to you; and to give thanks continuously. And because all things have contributed to your advancement, you should include all things in your gratitude.

Even in the presence of certain things you think are not good enough, learn to be grateful. Remember that they are all helping to arrange the lines of transmission along which your riches will come to you, and be grateful for them all. This will bring you into harmonious relations with the good in everything, and the good in everything will move towards you.

PERSONALITY FOR SUCCESS

It is the personalities at the back of a business which determines the measure of success the business will enjoy. Modify those personalities so they are more pleasing and more attractive to the patrons of the business and the business will thrive. People buy personalities as much as they buy physical goods and services. It is a question of whether they are influenced more by the personalities with which they come in contact than they are by the goods and services.

"Ninety-nine people out of every hundred who purchase life insurance policies do not know what is in their policies and do not seem to care. What they really purchase is the pleasing personality of some man or woman who knows the value of cultivating such a personality." It was stated earlier how thousands of men and women patronize music without the slightest understanding of the lyrics of the so called songs. Thousands attend churches or even social functions without being able to reflect on any part of the events shortly thereafter. All they know is the personalities behind such music or events. Millions of people put their money in the bank without a thought as to what the bank uses the money to do or where the bank keeps that money.

Your business in life, or at least the most important part of it, is to achieve success. Success, in this context, is the attainment of your Financial Goals without violating the rights of other people. Regardless of what your major aim in life may be, you will attain it with much less difficulty after you learn how to cultivate a pleasing personality and after you have learned the delicate art of aligning yourself with others in a given understanding without friction or envy. By this you secure a good place for yourself in the hearts of many who are important to facilitating your success in whatever form.

One of the greatest problems of life, if not, in fact, the greatest, is that of learning the art of harmonious negotiation with others. I have stated in this book the importance of compromise in the business and corporate journey. That was for the purpose of teaching people how to negotiate their way through life with harmony and poise, free from the destructive effects of disagreement and friction which bring millions of people to misery, want and failure in life.

You cannot enjoy outstanding success in life without power, and you can never enjoy power without sufficient personality to influence other people to cooperate with you in a spirit of harmony.

LIKE ATTRACTS LIKE

"If you are in business and have formed the habit of talking and thinking about "business being bad", business will be bad. One pessimist, provided he is permitted to continue his destructive influence long enough, can destroy the work of half a dozen competent men, and he will do it by setting a drift in the minds of his associates the thought of poverty and failure. Don't be this type of man or woman."

No business firm wants the services of a pessimist, and those who understand the Law of Attraction and Law of Habit will no more tolerate the pessimist than they would permit a burglar to roam around their place of business, for the reason that one such person will destroy the usefulness of those around him.

In tens of thousands of homes the general topic of conversation is poverty and want, and that is just what they are getting. They think of poverty, they talk of poverty, they accept poverty as their own lot in life. They reason that because their ancestors were poor before them they also must remain poor.

The poverty consciousness is formed as the result of the habit of thinking of and fearing poverty.

"YOU are a human magnet and you are constantly attracting to you people whose characters harmonize with your own.

Like attracts like, and you may see evidence of this law in every blade of grass and every growing tree. The oak attracts from the soil and the air the necessary materials out of which to grow an oak tree. It never grows a tree that is part oak and part poplar. Every grain of wheat that is planted in the soil attracts the materials out of which grow a stalk of wheat. It never makes a mistake and grows both oak and wheat on the same stalk.

Men are subject, also, to this same Law of Attraction. Go into any cheap nieghbourhood in any city and there you will find people of the same general trend of mind associated together. On the other hand, go into any prosperous community and there you will find people of the same general tendencies associated together. Men who are successful always seek the company of others who are successful, while men who are on the ragged side of life always seek the company of those who are in similar circumstances. "Misery love company."

Water seeks its level with no finer certainty than man seeks the company of those who occupy his own general status financially and mentally.

"You will attract to you people who harmonize with your own philosophy of life, whether you wish it or not"

DEFINITE FINANCIAL GOAL

True financial success involves personal choices. You cannot be rich as a result of economic accident. Success results only when opportunity is greeted with preparedness. Any fortune that comes to you without your preparedness is the fortune that will soon disappear. To be financially successful, you must have financial success as one of your chief goals. Your personal choice has the power to activate the inner resources from within you with which you can attain financial abundance.

The personal power from the inside of you has the force to attract all that you required for the attainment of your chief goals. All that you need are available in terms of materials, people and opportunities. They are all available in the world around you. Personal choice draws you to all that you need and draws all that you need to you. Personal choice also empowers you to be able to develop habits that naturally attract money making opportunities to you. These are parts of natural laws upon which our universe operates.

"It is most appalling to know that ninety-five per cent of the people of the world are drifting aimlessly through life, without the slightest conception of the work for which they are best fitted, and with no conception whatsoever of even the need of such a thing as a definite objective toward which to strive."

There is a psychological as well as an economic reason for the selection of a definite chief aim at every particular point in life. Napoleon Hill taught very well on the place of "Definite Chief Aim" in his "Law of Success Course"

Any definite chief aim that is deliberately fixed in the mind and held there, with the determination to realize it, finally saturates the entire subconscious mind until it automatically influences the physical action of the body toward the attainment of that purpose.

Your definite chief aim per time should be selected with deliberate care, and after it has been selected it should be written out and placed where you will see it at least once a day. The psychological effect of which is to impress this purpose upon your subconscious mind strongly that it accepts that purpose as a pattern or blueprint that will eventually dominate your activities in life and lead you, step by step, toward the attainment of the specific purpose.

"Be sure that your definite purpose is constructive, that its attainment will bring hardship and misery to no one; that it will bring you peace and prosperity, then apply to the limit of your understanding, the principle of self-suggestion for the speedy attainment of this purpose.

The subconscious mind may be likened to a magnet, and when it has been vitalized and thoroughly saturated with any definite purpose, it has a decided tendency to attract all that is necessary for the fulfillment of the purpose."

"There is much evidence to justify the belief that nothing within reason is beyond the possibility of attainment by the man whose definite chief am has been well developed."

SELF CONFIDENCE

Nothing can bring you success but yourself. Of Course you will need the co-operation of others if you aim to attain success of a far-reaching nature, but you will never get that cooperation unless you vitalize your mind with the positive attitude of self-confidence.

Perhaps you have wondered why a few men advance to

highly paid positions while others all around them, who have as much formal education and skills and who seemingly perform as much work, do not get ahead. Select any two people of these two types that you choose, and study them, and the reason why one succeeds and the other is not will be quite obvious to you. You will find that the one who advances believes in himself. You will find that he backs this belief with such dynamic, aggressive action that he lets others know that he believes in himself.

You will also find that the one who does not make necessary progress shows clearly, by the look on his face, by the posture of his body, by the lack of briskness in his steps, by the uncertainty with which he speaks, that he lacks Self-Confidence.

No one is going to pay much attention to the person who has no confidence in himself. He does not attract others because his mind is a negative force that repels rather than attracts. You must not only believe in yourself, you must also have absolute faith in the propriety of your definite purpose. You must assure yourself that God and His entire creation are at your support in the pursuit of your objective.

SELF CONFIDENCE FORMULA BY NAPOLEON HILL

You are advised to copy the following formula, sign it and commit it to memory.

First: I know that I have the ability to achieve the object of my definite purpose; therefore I demand of myself persistent, aggressive and continuous action toward its attainment.

Second: I realize that the dominating thoughts of my mind eventually reproduce themselves in outward, bodily action, and gradually transform themselves into physical reality, therefore I will concentrate my mind for thirty minutes daily upon the tasks of thinking of the person I intend to be, by creating a mental picture of this person and then transforming that picture into reality through practical service.

Third: I know that through the principles of Auto-Suggestion, any desire that I persistently hold in mind will eventually seek expression through some practical means of realizing it, therefore I shall devote ten minutes daily to demanding of myself the development of the factors necessary for the attainment of my positive desire.

Fourth: I have clearly mapped out and written down a description of my definite purpose in life, for the coming five years. I have set a price on my service for each of these five years; a price that I intend to earn and receive, through strict application of principle of efficient satisfactory service which I will render in advance.

Fifth: I fully realize that no wealth or position can long endure unless built upon truth and justice, therefore I will engage in no transaction which does not benefit all whom it affects. I will succeed by attracting to me the forces I wish to use, and the co-operation of other people. I will induce others to serve me because I will first serve them. I will eliminate hatred, envy, jealousy, selfishness and cynicism by developing love for all humanity, because I know that a negative attitude towards others can never bring me success. I will cause others to believe in me because I will believe in them and in myself.

I will sign my name to this formula, commit it to memory and repeat it aloud once a day with full faith that it will gradually influence my entire life so that I will become a successful and happy worker in my chosen field of endeavor.

TRUST

True success is impossible without trust. In every truly successful person is the capacity to trust and be trusted.

"One thing that is common to EVERY individual, friendship, relationship is that if you don't have trust, everything falls apart." **Stephen M. R Covey**

In the process of wealth creation, people will have to commit resources to you. In the same vein, you will have to commit resources to people. For this to happen, trust is very important. Trust means confidence. When we trust people, we have confidence in them - in their integrity and in their abilities.

Losing trust is losing money. All the money and other resources you are looking for are already in some people's hands. It is trust that attracts them to you.

When we distrust people, we are suspicious of them. Nobody commits resources to the hands of people of whom he is suspicious. If you hope to control resources, build trust. Develop a personality that can be trusted. People invest in personalities just the way they invest in companies and projects. You need a personality that can be invested in.

Wealth accumulation also requires your trusting in other people. This has to be done selectively and deliberately. It must be done all the same. Without trust in other people, you must be ready to live in corporate and financial isolation. That will mean your success depends largely only on your personal efforts. Personal efforts can only take you so far in the financial world. Real wealth comes when you are able to leverage on other people. You leverage on their strength, ability, knowledge, loyalty and even money. This requires trust.

"Relationships of all kinds are built on and sustained by trust. Trust in others depends on how much we trust ourselves". Stephen M.R. Covey

"Obviously no man would ever fear poverty if he had any grounds for trusting his fellow men, for there is food and shelter and raiment and luxury of every nature sufficient for the needs of every person except for the swinish habit that man has of trying to push all the other "swine" out of the trough, even after he has all and more than he needs." Napoleon Hill

"Trust men and they will be true to you; treat them greatly and they will show themselves great, though they make an exception in your favor to all their rules of trade." Napoleon Hill

TIME

"What you do with your time is a very big subject, because lost time can never be recaptured. Very often, lost money can be regained. As Plutarch said, "Time is the wisest of all counselors." In short, be careful of your time and learn to invest it thoughtfully" Donald J Trump.

Rich people value time more than anything else. They value time more than money. Time properly applied will generate all the money in this world. Truly wealthy people multiply their wealth by buying more time from other people. That is; in addition to the proper use of their own time, they buy more from other people's time. Each person on earth has twenty four hours each day. That is the most equitable thing in the world. That leaves nobody with any excuse. No excuse for failure in the long run.

"Until you value your life, you would not value your time and until you value your time, you would not do anything with it." M. Scott Peck

THE LAW OF TIME PERSPECTIVE

The law of time perspective says: "The most successful people in any society are those who take the longest time period into consideration when making their day to day decisions."

This insight comes from the pioneering work on upward financial mobility in America conducted by Dr. Edward Banfield of Harvard University in the late 1950s and early 1960s. After studying many of the factors that were thought to contribute to individual financial success over the course of a person's lifetime, he concluded that there was one primary factor that took precedence over all the others. He called it "time perspective".

What Banfield found was that the higher a person rises in any society, the longer the time perspective or time horizon of that person. People at the highest social and economic levels make decisions and sacrifices that may not pay off for many years, sometimes not even in their own lifetimes. Yet, they do it with all seriousness as if their lives depend on it. This is so powerful; that it is a prerequisite to quality leadership in all human endeavor.

It is equally important for financial leadership. I have illustrated in the previous chapters how this is a fundamental difference between the rich and the poor. The truly rich live for today and tomorrow. The poor practically live for today.

People with long time perspectives are willing to pay the price of success for a long, long time before they achieve it. They think about the consequences of their actions and their decisions in terms of what they might mean in five, ten, fifteen and even twenty years for now.

As you begin thinking longer term and organizing your life and priority with your future goals and ambitions in mind, the quality of your decisions improves and your life starts to become better almost immediately.

LEVERAGE

"Once you understand leverage, which is the ability to do more with less, you will probably begin to see leverage. At Rich Dad Company, I combine my talents with Kim's and Sharon's talents which give me much more leverage and is often called OPR-Other People's Resources. We use strategic partners to help us in several areas of our business, for instance we use a strategic partner to distribute our books so we do not have to build that capability inside Rich Dad. The important message is: Rich People use more leverage than poor people. If you want to be rich, you need leverage. If you want to be really

rich, you need a lot of leverage." Robert Kiyosaki. Leverage other people's money, other people's time, other people's talents and other resources.

ADAPTATION

This has to do with your ability to adjust your responses or reactions in line with changing economic and environmental demand. Different situations demand different responses. You must learn to change your responses without changing your principle and conviction. Learn to change your strategy as many times a necessary without changing your core objective. The propriety of the core objective is assumed to have been properly evaluated beforehand. Fanaticism is an enemy of progress, particularly in the changing world of today. The financial world requires a lot of compromise and adjustment. Learn to adjust based knowledge.

In a changing world, the learned are the worst for it while the learners are the better for it. The learned are those that live on the assumption that they already have enough knowledge in whatever sense. In a changing world, the learned continued to live in a world that no longer exists.

INDIFFERENCE

Rich people know what to ignore. They ignore many things that are not worthy of their attention. The rich select what they want and what they apply their energy and time to.

This is what most poor people find difficult to do. Poor people allow the environment to set agenda for them most of time.

In his magic ladder to success published in 1921, Napoleon Hill stated in the 9th point. "I enter into no arguments with people over trivial matters"

Poor people waste their time and energy on "trivial matters. Often time they get busy with things that do not have direct relevance to their lives. They allow the society to set agenda for them. Look around, you will discover that poor people are more involved in gossips. Poor people are more involved in spreading rumours. Whether you believe it or not, this will certainly reflect in their financial lives. You have only 24hours a day. What you apply the 24hours to is entirely your choice. However, that choice will directly impact your life. Particularly, it will affect your financial life.

You must be quick to identify things that are important to you. Allocate your effort based on the order of importance. This requires deliberate practice.

MONEY

"We are all affected by money, no matter who we are or where we live or what we do. Money like time, is a common denominator we share. Most people need money to buy food, which is necessary to sustain life, so they are

intertwined whether we choose to believe it or not.

Money will affect your life. My theory is that if something is going to affect your life, it's best to know as much as you can about it. Will you be able to find time to invest in your financial education?" Donald J. Trump

Rich people are able to acknowledge the importance of money in their lives. They also give it the attention it deserves. Poor people pretend about the importance of money. Yet they look for money 8am to 5pm on daily basis. The rich like money. The poor like money. However, the poor keep their like for money secret. The energy they are supposed to apply to legitimate money making is applied to keeping their desire for money secret. It is then difficult for them to concentrate. It is also difficult for them to convince their subconscious minds that they are doing the right thing by looking for money. Hence, their subconscious minds will find it difficult to go into active work in legitimate search for money.

RESPONSIBILITY

Expect more from yourself than anybody expects from you. You must also learn to expect more from yourself more than you expect from anybody else, as far as your financial life is concerned. Not even the government or your parents should be more responsible for your adult life than yourself. The moment you take responsibility for everything in your life, you can change everything in your life.

Rich people take responsibility for the outcomes of their lives. Poor people look for whom to blame for their failures.

SKILLS

The place of skills cannot be overemphasized. Many people complain of lack of opportunities. Others lament of lack of money or capital. The real problem, many of the times is the lack of skills. Productive skill is very important. Money will follow after good skills. It takes skills to get the problems solved. Money follows after problem solving. Reputation, honour and respect follow after the man that solves problems. Before you need money you need skills. Even after you have gotten money you still need skills.

There is a stage of life that acquiring necessary skill should be what matters to you. When we were in our primary and secondary schools, money making was not necessarily a priority to majority of us. All you need was to concentrate on your studies and pass your examinations well. That was then enough definition of success. The idea behind that was that you devote such a time of your life to learning- learning skills. It is believed that you will later in life use the skills to earn money.

Unfortunately, school training nowadays is not geared towards practical and specific skills that can naturally enable you to solve life's problems in a way to earn money. In the industrial era, school training was largely adequate to give people necessary basic skills and prepare them to learn further skills on the job. Many of today's curricula are still tailored after the industrial era schemes. Meanwhile, the major problem of the Industrial era which was mass production of articles has been solved by technology. Yet our school curricular are still built with the orientation of the Industrial age. Therefore, many come out of school without specific problem solving skills. The school system conditions most students to be able to memorise and recite without specific application to practical life problems. Even the technical courses today hardly prepare their students to be productive after school. Therefore, you must address your mind to the fact that being a university graduate does not necessarily indicate that you have productive skills.

Before thinking of money making, evaluate yourself as to what particular skills do you have and what particular problems can you solve with them. This has to be done with all sincerity to yourself. If you find out you don't have skills that people are ready to pay for, quickly go and learn one. You can also learn more than one. There are people with skills that were once in high demand but today the tide has changed. As a beginner, you can learn a number of skills. Later in life you will narrow down to one or a few. Experience will certainly point you to the one to concentrate on. As you grow in life, concentration becomes more and more important.

Money is a means of exchange. Money is what comes to you directly or indirectly for the value you created or problems you solve for other people and the society. It is skill that you use to solve problems. It is skills that you use to create value. Therefore, for you to attract money, you must think of problem solving. You must think in terms of value adding. For you to add value and solve problem, you must think in terms of productive and sellable skills.

There are physical skills like the ones the engineers use on construction sites. Technical, engineering, mechanical, vocational and technological skills are always physical in nature. There are other skills referred to as "soft skills". These have become more and more important in the society of today. While the physical skills are about how you use the nonliving things and non-human agents in getting specific problems solved and creating desired values, soft skills are about the use of interpersonal human relation to create a better world and better environment. The point here is that people must know that both physical and soft skills are important and both are teachable and learnable. With the world becoming a global village, soft skills have gained more importance nowadays.

The following are examples of soft skills:
Persuasion
Persuasive Business presentation
Teamwork and collaboration
Business Intuition

Conflict resolution
Diplomacy
Adaptability
Critical Observation etc.

Possession of skills alone is not likely going to make anyone rich. But right skill is a necessary tool that will accelerate your journey to riches. You must possess the right skills and such skills must be properly and rightly deployed. There must also be an alignment between your physical skills, soft skills and natural talents. Your skills also must align with the need of your economic environment. It must be the one that must be able to provide solution that is required by the society. No one pays for your skills, people only pay for the solution that you provide to their problems using your skills.

PERSUASION

You are in the people's world. Ability to persuade other people to your line of thought is very critical to financial success. You practically have to become a salesman of some sort. Even when you are in a technical field, you cannot generate significant wealth or make notable impact without been able to persuade other people to support you in the pursuit of your business objectives. Even as an employee, you will need to be able to persuade both your subordinates and your superiors on critical issues. Without this you cannot grow on the job.

You will need to persuade customers. You will need to persuade investors as well as partners. Persuasion ability is money that can be tapped with appropriate knowledge. It is a skill that must be learned. It is a skill that you must continue to cultivate and improve upon, if you ever dream of building sustainable wealth.

RELATIONSHIP

At certain level in life, relationship is the greatest thing that you need in your financial life. At that stage the importance of other things that had been the drivers of your financial life continue to go down while that of "purposeful relationships" continue to grow. There is a time in your life that even skills cannot help you that much. If you enter into financial crisis at age 50 for instance, skill is not likely going to solve your problem. At that time, it is a function of the type of relationship you have cultivated over the years. At that age, no one is looking for your technical ability any more. There are thousands of younger people with the same technical ability and more energy than you probably have.

At that age, you have people around you who can make telephone calls that will turn your situation around. At 50, you should have people who can stake large amounts of money for the relationship they share with you. At that point in life, you should know and have relationship with a number of people that matter in the society. You must also be someone that can be there for other people in time of trouble. When people are broke at age 50, their problem is not likely a money problem. It is not likely a skill problem. It is most likely a relationship problem. As you grow in life, your association matters. Your roles in the society matters. Your neighborhood matters. I have dealt a lot with this in the discussions on internal and external environments.

There are people who are happy being local champions. Part of the problems with this is that they will find it difficult to have people around that can lift them up when they fall or have some setback. The financially intelligent people don't only build relationship for today. They build relationship for their financial future. This is one of the reasons some progressive organizations sponsor their executive in the membership of some reputable social and professional organizations. Unfortunately, many executives don't know why. And many others don't bother to ask why. To your financial life, where you work, where you live, the church you belong to, your family name and your social and professional associations matter. All of these relationship can be built. They can be cultivated. They can be purposefully developed. Always do your best to establish, keep, maintain and nourish valuable relationships.

Of course, there are certain relationships you need to take intentional steps to terminate. These are relationships that are not adding value to your life. All relationships must be evaluated on a continual basis. There are relationships that were once valuable and productive, but your current evaluation shows they are no longer profitable. You must be ready to terminate such relationships. It take very strong emotional maturity to be able to put an end to a relationship you once enjoyed. But you must realize that this is part of life. Certain relationships are not meant for a life time. Financially intelligent People know this so well. Successful politicians also seem to work with this consciousness. They believe there are no permanent friends or enemies. There are only permanent interests. Relationships could be casual, cordial or intimate. Each of them has its own role. Each must be consciously established, developed and nurtured.

POWER

Money answers to power. Most people know this. Africans believe money answers to power, with focus on spiritual power, political power, royal power and position power and so on. I have some level of belief along these lines too. I believe money to some extent answer to spiritual power. Likewise political power and other forms of power.

However, I believe all human possess some levels of power naturally. And that is the basic anyone needs to attract money. To start with, all men have some level of spiritual power. Being conscious of such power is another thing. Learning the right use of such power is also very important. A combination of all the powers required to achieve greatness is embedded in every man. Therefore, there is no acceptable excuse for poverty or low life.

As stated earlier, all the forces in God's Creation are meant for your success. They are for you and not against you. Your ability to believe this fact is very important. You also need to know that you can consciously mobilize these forces to support your just course. Do I mean some kind of divination or something of such? No. You can turn the forces of the universe to your favour by conducting your life in the ways that have been recommended in this book, particularly those principles summarized in this chapter and the last. They are natural principles that are meant to support any dweller of the earth who is determined in the pursuit of a just course. They work within the universal laws.

You are an embodiment of power. And the discussion on power is more than a topic for this chapter. I want to briefly mention four types of power you need to learn to leverage on, no matter your level or status in life. When properly leveraged, they will move you from where you are to where you ought to be, in a matter of time. These powers are either available to you or you can get them if you so determine and plan to that effect.

1. Personal Power
2. Organizational Power
3. Industrial Power
4. Societal Power

Power can accelerate your journey to financial success. Each person is born with some innate personal power qualities. It is the responsibility of each person to discover, cultivate and develop such power. Deployment of personal power is fundamental to acquisition and sustenance of wealth. Personal power naturally attracts opportunities to the one that deploys it wisely. My objective is to provide a brief explanation on "Personal Power" while I hope to deal with the four forms of power listed above in my subsequent book.

PERSONAL POWER

Personal Power is "**power that is intrinsic to the person who has it. It's based upon a person's personal qualities and traits, such as honesty, courage, heroism or the ability to inspire**" Study.com

"Personal Power is the source of the influence and authority a person has over his or her followers."
"Influence over others, the source of which resides in the person instead of being vested by the position he or she holds."

We have stated earlier the fact that we live in the world of people. All the money you need in this world is already in the hands of people. All you need is the ability to get them to release the money to you legitimately. You must offer them value for which they will be ready to part with their money.

However, it is not only about the quality of the value you offer that makes people to release their money to you. It is also about your personality that convey the value. Cultivating a strong personality is therefore a vital part of lasting wealth building. The good news is that anyone can decide to cultivate a strong personal power. You can decide to become and remain a person of influence even at your level. Personal power can be monetized over time.

Even as a taxi driver, Obafemi Awolowo was a very strong personality. Many people knew him as a lawyer and a politician. He was at different times:

1. Journalist
2. Teacher
3. Clerk
4. Money Lender
5. Produce Broker
6. Lawyer
7. Politician
8. Taxi Driver

My resent studies shows that the legendary Obafemi took positions of leadership and influence while he was in each of these trades. All these contributed to whatever he would later become.

LEARNING

Intelligent people in any area of human endeavour are not

people who know everything in that area. They are people who have the capacity and the commitment to learn. Wealthy people are always committed to lifelong learning. This is more important in our today's rapidly changing world. If you want to build sustainable wealth, you must possess the right attitude to learning. There is always something to learn, formally or informally.

As you grow, learning becomes more and more informal. Even when you attend formal trainings, the methodology must be with the use of a lot of informal approach and tools. In January 2017, I attended a coaching class organised by Reverend Sam Adeyemi's Success Power Organisation. The fee for the two day course was N500, 000.00 (Five Hundred Thousand Naira Only). Many of my mates would rather use such an amount for other things than pay it for a two day training. It is all about our value system. The knowledge and the connection from that training will give me the course fee many times over if properly used.

A friend told me something more than a decade ago. He was (still is) an executive in one of the new generation banks in Nigeria. Then, banking experience was highly valued and well recognized in the Nigerian labour Market. He said it is possible for someone to spend ten years in the bank as employee whereas his total banking experience is not more than three years equivalent. He went on to say that it is also possible to work for three years in the bank and gather working experience equivalent of ten years. I agree with him. It is all about your attitude to learning and the actual learning.

RESPONSIBILITY

Ability and willingness to take responsibility is very important to achievement of success in any area of life, particularly in finances. The problem with many poor and average people is their attitude of non-willingness to take responsibility. Most of the actions and decisions that result in money making also have the inherent possibility of resulting in losses. The right attitude is to be ready to take responsibility for either of the possible outcomes. Avoiding one is avoiding the other.

The other aspect of accepting responsibility is being ready to identify with specific problem by being ready to pay the price for the solution. Money follows problem solving. Whereas, the nature of man is to abhor problems. But no problem is ever solved by running away from it. No problem is ever solved by avoiding it. Problem is solved only by confronting it. If you want to be rich, you must learn to confront problems particularly when majority try to avoid it. That route most times is a lonely one but you must be ready to travel it.

LOYALTY

Loyalty is an asset. It is an asset to the one that is loyal and also to the recipient of loyalty. You must understand that loyalty is a commodity. People pay for loyalty. The financially intelligent understand this. They are ready to buy loyalty at appropriate prices. They are also ready to maintain loyalty towards people who deserve it and are expected to be able to pay for it.

Loyalty should be a two way thing. The one that receive loyalty must be ready to give loyalty. It is ignorance that makes some people expect to receive loyalty without being ready to give loyalty in return. Some also believe that it is the junior ones that must be loyal to the senior. Nothing can be farther from the truth. The seniors are also expected to be loyal to their worthy juniors. Loyalty must be give and take.

You must be sure your loyalty is not misplaced. Don't be loyal to somebody you are sure is not capable of being loyal to you in return. It may be very difficult to establish someone's ability in this regard beforehand. Loyalty therefore involves some elements of risk. Continuous evaluation of your important relationships in this regard is important. As soon as you discover that your loyalty has been misplaced, make adjustments immediately.

Loyalty must be bought either with money or value of any other form.

LANGUAGE

Your language is a major determinant of the ultimate outcome of your life. The rich have their language. They have their own vocabulary. The poor also have their language. One of the first steps to being rich is to learn the language of the rich.

You don't need to have money for you to learn and speak like the rich. You only need to learn the language and the money will come.

Your language shapes your entire life. It determines the type of people you will attract. Your language determines the type of things that will happen in your life frequently. It is difficult to speak like a rich man while you wallow in poverty. It is however more difficult to change your life without changing your language.

EXPOSURE

Exposure makes big things become common. It moves issues from being strange to being familiar. Lack of familiarity makes even simple things look difficult. Exposure makes difficult things look simple. This is one major way travelling and tourism have direct impact on our financial lives. Your social and business association are also very important.

Learn to hang around people who are getting things done.

Associate with people who are already doing that which you are planning to achieve. Read about achievers. Form the picture in your mind of how they are getting things done. Visualize yourself getting it done just like them. Visit countries, cities and neighborhoods that are more developed than yours. Visit companies and possibly homes of achievers. This makes greatness become common in your mind. Anything you have not seen before is naturally a mystery to you. Exposure helps demystify things. It demystifies issues. It draws dreams closer to reality.

SOCIETY

One major problem of most developing countries is that of having few rich men in poor society. There is a societal dimension to true wealth. It is doubtful whether those few rich people in very poor societies can be regarded as rich people. **First**, it is very difficult to enjoy wealth in the mist of extremely poor populace. There is also the tendency to assume you are rich when you are actually not. Many people who are being celebrated as rich in many African societies today are mere local champions. At most, they are middle class people.

If you dream of being rich, the development of your society must be very important to you. As you dream of the type of life you desire to live, you must also dream of the type of society you want to live in. That will propel you to a higher standard of financial life and practices. It will also set the platform for you to enjoy your wealth. Jack Ma is one of the richest in the world today. He is actually the richest in China. I heard him recently saying that man is not on earth to make money. Rather, man is on earth to enjoy. How you enjoy your money is as important as how you make your money. Therefore, society matters.

"We are in this together, is a better philosophy than you are on your own" Bill Clinton

DECISION

Decision is the forerunner of every worthwhile success. Ability to take decision and stick to the decision, even in the face of all odds and difficulties is the hallmark of truly successful people. They don't jump at decisions without deep thought. Likewise, they don't jump out just because it has become difficult.

Human life is designed in such a way that you cannot do without decision making. There are good decisions which will always lead to good results "in the long run". Bad decisions will lead to failure "in the long run". The truth is that we all make a number of decisions on a daily bases. Some of the decisions are very central and important to our lives' outcomes. Others are less important. Intelligence is to attach the right value to your decisions. It is also the ability to learn to make conscious decisions in order to avoid the accidents of life. In reality, most of the things people call accidents are actually the results of wrong decisions. Failure to make decision is already a decision. It is that important.

For instance, a man without a decision to succeed has already made decision to fail. He has done so unconsciously. Many people run away from decision making because of fear of failure. Behind fear of failure is lack of readiness to take responsibility for possible wrong outcome of a decision. It is however better to make wrong decision unknowingly than to refuse to make decision at all. The man that makes decision has two possibilities ahead of him. The man that avoids decision making has only one certain outcome ahead of him. The man that makes decision has the possibilities of success or failure. The one without decision is guaranteed to fail.

There cannot be such thing as accidental wealth. A decision to be rich is a must. It precedes any true wealth. You must also note that decision making is an art. It can be cultivated. It can be learnt. If you hope to be rich someday, you need to learn the "art of financial decision making". We are in a world where majority don't make financial decisions. They leave their financial lives to destiny. Some leave that to the society or the government. Others leave theirs to their wealthy parents. Living in such a society will make you look odd if you want to take decisions and live by them. You may lose your societal acceptance or even face outright persecution. Society generally wants to lead you. They set the status quo and expect everyone to keep to it. Strong and successful people have learnt to challenge the status quo.

Until you learn to make financial decisions and take responsibility for the decisions, your chances of being rich is very slim. This is also applicable to success in all other areas of life. As you learn to make financial decisions devoid of sentiments, your chances of financial success and wealth building increases.

www.ingramcontent.com/pod-product-compliance
Lightning Source LLC
Chambersburg PA
CBHW071431230926
51846CB00001B/182
* 9 7 8 9 7 8 9 6 4 8 6 7 2 *